Excel Basic Skills

Comprehension and Written Expression

Year 7
Ages 12-13

Get the Results You Want!

Alan Horsfield

Reprinted 2000, 2001, 2002, 2004, 2005, 2007, 2008, 2012

Updated in 2013 for the Australian Curriculum

Reprinted 2015, 2017, 2020, 2023

ISBN 978 1 86441 379 3

Pascal Press
PO Box 250
Glebe NSW 2037
(02) 9198 1748
www.pascalpress.com.au

Publisher: Vivienne Joannou
Project editor: Mark Dixon
Text design and typesetting by Scriptorium Desktop Publishing Pty Ltd
Additional typesetting by Grizzly Graphics (Leanne Richters)
Australian Curriculum updates edited by Frances Wade
Cover by Dizign Pty Ltd
Printed by Vivar Printing/Green Giant Press

Acknowledgements

Elaine Horsfield of EJH Talent Promotion P/L for support and assistance with question sets
Kylie Lowson (Pascal Press) who braved the tyrannies of distance and (Fiji) time to make it all happen

Antarctica by John Collerson, The Spectrum Series, HBJ, 1992
Book Review—Code of Deception by Alan Horsfield from *Magpies* Magazine, 1996
Bush Medicine by Konai Helu-Thaman from Langakali, The South Pacific Creative Arts Society. Reproduced with SPCAS permission
Circles by William Taylor, Penguin Books (NZ), Auckland 1996
Earth First by David Bowden and Jenny Dibley, The Spectrum Series, HBJ, 1992
For Better or For Worse by Lynn Johnson, © United Features Syndicate
Hagar the Horrible by Dik Browne. Reproduced with the kind permission of King Features Syndicate © 1999 King Features Syndicate, ™ The Hearst Corporation
Iga Warta ad reproduced with the kind permission of Iga Warta .
'"Indian" war club (the tale of three Lovoni men)' from *Fiji Magic,* August 1998, Suva, Fiji
Land of the Rippling Gold by Una Clarke, The Spectrum Series, HBJ, 1992
Lawn Local by Suellen Sales
'Marauding elephants feel the heat' by Jonathan Beard from *New Scientist*, Vol. 154, No. 2087 (19 April 1997)
'Mystery at Mandurah—water under the bridge' by Jill Burgess, South West Publishing, *Mandurah Telegraph*
Night of the Muttonbirds by Mary Small, The Spectrum Series, HBJ, 1992
Odious Underarmus, Marathon Man by Bill Condon and Dianne Bates from *Stagestruck*, The Spectrum Series, HBJ, 1992
'"Old faithful" erupts in space' by Jeff Hecht from *New Scientist*, 2 December 1995 (p. 5)
Perfect Timing by Jeremy Fisher, The Spectrum Series, HBJ, 1992
Pets, the Law and You in NSW by Karen Don for Humane Society International Inc., Sydney 1996
Polar Ice from *The Earth* by QL Pearce, Playmore Inc., RGA Publishing Group, New York, 1989
Politically Correct by Greg Anderson-Clift
Roland Harvey's Book of Christmas by Roland Harvey, Roland Harvey Books, Port Melbourne
Shaping the News by John D Fitzgerald, The Spectrum Series, HBJ, 1991
Special Day by David Bateson, 1977
Sport in the Making by Shane Power, The Spectrum Series, HBJ, 1990
Springtime on Mars adapted from Malin Space Science Mission: http://www.msss.com/mars/global_surveyor/camera/
Streetscape by Ian Steep from *Through the Web and Other Stories*, The Spectrum Series, HBJ, 1992
Technology for the Environment by Mike Callaghan and Peter Knapp, The Spectrum Series, HBJ, 1992
That's a Job for Me! by Ross Pearce, The Spectrum Series, HBJ, 1992
The Age of Dinosaurs in Australia by Tim Flannery and Paula Kendall, The Spectrum Series, HBJ, 1990
The Incredible Experience of Megan Kingsley by Pamela O'Connor, The Spectrum Series, HBJ, 1990
The Tommy Tycho Story by Tommy Tycho, Brolga Publishing, Ringwood, Victoria, 1995
The Tree of Life by The Coconut Board, Ministry of Agriculture, Fiji
Touch and Feeling by Robert Royston, Macdonald Educational, Great Britain, 1985
Warbirds over Wanaka by Shiri Gounder from *Islands*, Vol. 3, 1998, Suva, Fiji
'What authors get when a book is sold' from *Australian Author*, Vol. 30, No. 2, 1998, Strawberry Hills
'Why shopping trips end in tears for kids' by Vincent Kiernan from *New Scientist,* 2 December 1995 (p. 5)

All efforts to contact individuals regarding copyright have been made and permission acknowledged where applicable. Apologies to authors for accidental infringement where copyright has been untraceable. The publishers would appreciate any information on accurate copyright details.

Contents

To Parents and Teachers

When the student completes the exercises in this book he or she will have worked through a number of question types from a variety of text types.

Rather than give a range of question types based on each passage, the focus in this book will be on developing the student's skill with a particular question type. The book is so structured that if there is a weakness in a particular skill then the student can concentrate on that and become competent without working through passages and questions that may not contribute to his or her progress.

Each new section provides information on what is required for the particular skill being practised. Generally, the first extract/passage in each section is intended to lead the student through a number of questions based upon a specific skill. A full set of answers is provided in the middle of the book.

This book uses a range of text types so that the student will feel confident in a variety of situations. Text types are usually broken into two broad types—literary and factual. Within each group are numerous varieties—some are listed below. (A more comprehensive explanation is found on page 1.)

Literary texts include narratives (novels/stories), poetry and (drama) scripts.

Factual texts include explanations, expositions, information reports, recounts and procedures.

As you can see, the range is quite extensive. It is important that students develop comprehension skills from a variety of text types. Many types of writing overlap.

On several occasions extracts are reused. This is done to demonstrate that different comprehension skills can be developed from the same piece of writing. Comprehension skills are interdependent.

As the student's ability to comprehend increases he or she will also be expected to interpret data. This includes the interpretation of information found in charts, in tables and on maps.

Question types include questions that require (not in any specific order):

- true or false responses
- multiple-choice responses
- short-answer responses
- full-sentence answers
- matching skills
- sentence completing
- sequencing skills
- open-ended responses
- giving reasons
- cloze skills (filling in blanks)
- language knowledge
- giving opinions and justifying them
- predicting skills
- labelling skills
- inferring skills
- interpreting data
- recognising 'audience'
- discussing theme/plot
- recognising purpose
- understanding shades of meaning.

It is suggested that students resist the temptation to give unnecessarily short answers. Such answers can be misinterpreted by markers. To the marker who is not sure of the student's intent, such answers can be ambiguous.

Good luck!

Alan Horsfield

Text Types—An Overview

A text is any meaningful **written** or **spoken** message. It is communication. In writing or speaking we can create texts and by reading and listening we can understand and interpret texts.
Text types are often called genres. Text types can be classified in a number of ways. The following classification has been adapted from *Pascal's Basic Primary Grammar* by P Walker (Pascal Press, 1996).
Text types are often broadly classified into two basic types: **literary** and **factual**.

Literary Texts

Narratives	Drama	Poetry
examples are		
Novels Stories Myths/Legends Science Fiction Fantasy Tables Jokes	Stage Plays Film Scripts Radio Scripts	Limericks Lyrics Sonnets Nonsense rhymes Poems Songs Jingles

Text types can overlap. For example, a stage play may be written in verse.
Try these questions.

1. Name a famous playwright who wrote plays in verse. ______________________
2. In which column would you put **comics**? ______________________
3. What is your reason? ______________________

Factual Texts

Discussions	Explanations	Expositions	Information Reports	Procedures	Recounts
examples are					
Debates Talkback Radio Discussions	Textbooks Scientific Writing Spoken Presentations	Advertisements Lectures Editorials Speeches Letters to Editors Newspaper Cartoons	Documentaries Announcements Reference Books Guide Books	Instructions Directions Recipes Tables of Events	Diaries Newspapers Reports Historical Reports Letters Logs Timelines

No doubt more examples of text types can be added to this list.
Factual text types, too, can overlap. A historical recount may be presented as a TV play.
Interpreting data is an important skill in modern society. Data may include graphs, timetables, flow charts, maps and labelled diagrams.
Try these questions.

1. Name a famous writer of a diary. ______________________
2. In which column would you put **postcards**?______________________
3. What is your reason? ______________________
4. In what group would you put a **poster** for a Walt Disney film? ______________________
5. What is your reason? ______________________

Understanding Questions—Hypnotism

In your comprehension exercises you will get many different types of questions. Different types of questions are used to see how well you read and **comprehend** what you have read.

- Questions that want you to **find information** may begin with *How*, *When*, *Where* or *What*. Sometimes you will be asked to give **names**, make **lists** or even **label** diagrams.
- Questions that want you to **give a reason** will often begin with *Why*.
- Some questions may ask you to **give an opinion**. For these questions you need to have your own ideas and you should **answer in your own words** based upon information available or your understanding of a topic. For these question there is really no right or wrong answer as long as you can give an adequate reason.
- Other questions may ask you to **search and find** information in the text, especially in factual texts.

Read the following extract and answer the questions.

What do you really understand about hypnotism? More to the point, what do you believe?

Have you ever seen a hypnotist on television, making people quack like ducks or sing like Elvis, and wondered, 'Can hypnotists really make you do something you wouldn't normally do?' or 'Can a hypnotist really control your mind?' Well, psychologists have the answer.

Based upon what they have seen on television, at the movies and during stage shows that feature hypnosis, many believe that hypnosis can be used to control people without their consent. It has been reported that last century people who committed crimes, supposedly under the influence of an unscrupulous hypnotist, were not legally responsible for their actions.

Recent research by psychologists tells us that a response to hypnotic suggestion is not due to the powers of the hypnotist, but to the talent and willingness of the hypnotised person—the volunteer.

1. What does the author suggest is the truth behind hypnotism? (A full sentence answer is required.)

____.

2. Draw a line to match each sentence beginning with its correct ending.

TV show volunteers	has cast doubt on the popularly held beliefs.
Research by psychologists	are often willing to be hypnotised.
Hypnotists	are generally believed to have special powers.

3. **True or false?** Hypnotists make people commit crimes. ☐ True ☐ False (Tick one box.)

4. **Sentence completion:** A response to hypnotic suggestion is due to ________________________

____.

5. **Opinion:** Do you think people should be hypnotised to act in an embarrassing way? ____________

What is your reason? ____

____

____

Understanding Questions—Freeflyers: Modern Skydivers

Imagine falling towards the planet Earth at a terrifying 300 kilometres per hour. You started your fall from over four kilometres above the Earth. And you have less than one minute before you pull your parachute cord. You are falling so fast that just turning your head can send you off in a different direction. This is the wild side of a sport that has not found its limits—freeflying.

Freeflying is a variation on the more **traditional** skydiving. Skydivers are groups of jumpers who create magnificent, often very difficult manoeuvres in free fall. With skydiving, all the jumpers are travelling at the same speed in the same arena of activity. They create formations and movements that make the onlookers gape in awe.

Even experienced skydivers watch the antics of freeflyers in amazement. The skill and control of a freeflyer leaves many formation flyers shaking their heads.

Freeflyers, as the name suggests, do not hang around in crowds. Freeflyers enjoy the more spontaneous thrill of doing their own thing.

The wildest trip for a freeflyer is falling 'head down'. You are heading straight to earth head first! falling 'head first' requires a great deal of control—and nerve. The small surface presented to the air means that not only do you travel faster but the slightest movement has a greater effect on your direction.

Even the gear of freeflyers is more **outrageous**. They wear the zaniest jumpsuits, outlandish helmets and smaller 'chutes. In fact their 'chutes are about one quarter the size of the traditional skydiver's 'chute, which means they surf to the ground at about sixty kilometres per hour.

It is only in the last few years that freeflying has gained any real public acceptance.

1. **Opinion**: Which of the two activities—skydiving or freeflying—do you think would be the most dangerous? ______________ Briefly give your reason. ______________________________

____

Search and find: Write **short answers** (one or two words) for questions 2 to 4.

2. How fast do freeflyers fall before they use their 'chute? ______________________
3. How long do freeflyers drop for before pulling the cord? ______________________
4. What activity are skydivers most interested in? ______________________
5. **True or false?** Most people find skydiving a spectacular sport. ☐ True ☐ False
6. **Inferring**: Freeflyers could best be described as (impudent disorganised daring).
7. **Reasoning**: Skydiving requires more cooperation of participants than freeflying does because

   ____.
8. **Language**: The word *outrageous* could best be replaced by (shocking sensational).
9. **Language**: Which of the following words is closest in meaning to the word *traditional*, as used in the passage? (historical reliable conventional cautious) (Circle one.)
10. **Audience**: This passage would most likely be found in a manual teaching people how to freefly.

    ☐ True ☐ False

Understanding Questions—Cloze Exercises

Cloze exercises can have a variety of purposes. They can test your understanding of grammatical features of language, they can test your word knowledge or they can test your comprehension of an extract.

In **cloze exercises** you have to select the best word to fill (**close**) the space. To do cloze exercises well you should read the title of the extract, if there is one, and the whole extract and look at any graphics before beginning. When you have completed the exercise read it through again, from the beginning, to ensure it makes sense. It can help to mouth the words as you read them.

Read these extracts and answer the questions. This is a grammar/spelling type exercise. (Circle the correct letter—don't write in the spaces.)

As he ran for the school bus he felt great, not just because he was getting away from school and going home after a difficult day, ___(1)___ because the run itself was exhilarating. It was a break from that prison they called school. The driver smiled as he jumped to the steps just as the door closed and he said, "Made it!"

He was surprised when she replied. "You look as if you just escaped ___(2)___ a gang of kidnappers."

People in Sydney don't make light conversation any more, he thought. Haven't got the time. Or too scared they'll get reported for something silly, like being friendly. His smile widened as the bus pulled into the line of traffic.

Things ___(3)___ looking better already.

1. (A) or
(B) but
(C) and
(D) yet

2. (A) off
(B) into
(C) from
(D) away

3. (A) is
(B) are
(C) was
(D) were

This time consider the meanings of the words and the context in which they are used.
Read this extract from *Streetscape* by Ian Steep and answer the questions.

At the outdoor cafe people sat ___(4)___ over small tables to chat, or stretched back and read newspapers; the winter sunshine more important than their coffee and cakes.

It was already late morning and Michael was hungry. He kept moving to ___(5)___ suspicion, walking slowly past shop windows examining the ___(6)___. Harry's cafe was reflected in the glass. A couple of girls Michael knew had settled themselves on a planter box near the tables, and were **slyly** observing the customers.

A taxi turned the corner and pulled into the kerb. A smartly dressed woman reached forward to pay the driver then she pushed open the taxi door. As she stepped onto the pavement the girls made their ___(7)___. As carelessly as hurried shoppers, as carefully as jewel thieves, they moved towards the woman. It was all over before anyone saw what had happened.

4. (A) slumped
(B) huddled
(C) stranded
(D) crowded

5. (A) avoid
(B) dodge
(C) baffle
(D) report

6. (A) scene
(B) exhibit
(C) displays
(D) evidence

7. (A) bid
(B) move
(C) action
(D) proposal

8. The word *slyly* means ☐ 'in a criminal manner'. ☐ 'with stealth'. ☐ 'slowly'.

Understanding Questions—Multiple-Choice Questions

Read the extract from William Taylor's book *Circles* and answer the **multiple-choice questions**. Circle one letter for questions 1 to 4. Question 5 is a **sequencing** question.
Note: in extracts where the name of the storyteller is not known, he or she is often referred to as the narrator.

My mother died of sick madness. She died of this sick madness and of grief and fear. She died in a strange and alien place, so far from what she thought of as home, a home she would never, ever see again.

If a story may be said to have a beginning, this is the beginning of mine. In truth, I know, the story of no one really does have a beginning. There must always be something that has just gone on before and there were, naturally, a lot of somethings that happened before my mother's death that indeed led to that cursed and dreadful moment. It is true, though, that the dying of the poor sad woman I loved so dearly really did provide the marker, the turning point to my subsequent existence.

It was fifty years ago to the day, the day on which I choose to begin to write these words, fifty years ago that my father, my brother and I dug her grave, dressed Mother in her own good gown, wrapped her remains, poor thin little soul she had become, in the linen that had once been her mother's, and laid her to rest among those trees. At rest in those trees, beneath the trees she had so greatly feared. She rests there today, a scant half mile from where I sit writing these words, words that I write surrounded by a comfort and splendour that she never experienced and of which, likely, simple soul, she never dreamed.

Today I pushed my way through the undergrowth, doing my best to follow the ill-formed track to the spot beneath the giant rimu tree where a slab of marble says: Elizabeth Costello 1840–1876 and John Costello 1839–1876. My father, foolish man, lost spirit, survived his wife by no more than a handful of hours. Robert and I dug his grave and then we left this place with, in reality, little hope of ever seeing it again.

1. Elizabeth Costello could best be described as living
- (A) a life of sorrow and desperation.
- (B) a simple and bountiful country life.
- (C) surrounded by comfort and splendour.
- (D) in the one place for the whole of her life.

2. Fifty years before the narrator started writing
- (A) he left home, never expecting to return.
- (B) his brother was buried under the trees.
- (C) his parents arrived in a strange and alien land.
- (D) he revisited his parents' graves for the first time.

3. The narrator's return to his parents' graves had been
- (A) planned well in advance.
- (B) undertaken many times.
- (C) something he'd thought he couldn't do.
- (D) in the company of his brother.

4. This extract, most likely, originally came from
- (A) a manual.
- (B) a historical recount.
- (C) a teenagers' magazine.
- (D) a review.

5. Write the numbers 1 to 4 in the boxes to show the sequence of events in the extract.
- ☐ John Costello dies.
- ☐ The sons dig their mother's grave.
- ☐ The narrator begins his writing.
- ☐ Elizabeth Costello leaves her childhood home.

Note: read the extract softly to yourself to see if your sequencing makes sense.

Finding Facts—Polar Ice

When finding facts you will often be asked questions beginning with *Who*, *When*, *Where*, *What* and *How*, and sometimes *Why*. You will be asked to search for answers to questions that help you understand the **time** (**when**) and **place** (**where**) of the action in the extract, as well as **who** or **what** is involved. *Which* may also be used. Sometimes you will be asked to **give names** or **make lists**.

You will be expected to find facts in both factual material and narratives (stories). In factual material, important points may be introduced with bullet points (•).

Many exercises in this part of the book are based upon factual writing. 'Polar Ice', an extract from *The Earth* by QL Pearce, is a good place to start looking for facts. Generally you should answer with full-sentence answers unless asked to do otherwise. Full-sentence answers help you to focus on what the question is actually asking.

Now read the extract.

Polar Ice

We have all seen those beautiful documentaries on television which provide viewers with brilliant pictures of the South Polar region—stark white landscapes and seascapes against a backdrop of crisp blue skies. The Antarctic is a special place of ice and snow. It is the ice and snow that make it so spectacular.

When salt water freezes it is called pack ice. The cold winds of the polar regions chill the sea water until it forms plates of ice crystals called frazel ice. The thin frazel ice sheets on the surface are usually broken up by water movement into large irregular discs, or **pancake ice**. Further freezing creates a solid slab called an ice floe. New ice floes are two to three metres thick. If they do not melt away in summer they refreeze in winter, becoming even thicker. Seas of pack ice widen in winter and recede in summer, but the polar regions have huge areas of permanent pack ice. Special ships, called icebreakers, can often plough through these frozen seas.

In the Antarctic, layers of snow on land are compressed into huge rivers of ice. These rivers of ice, glaciers, flow towards the sea at speeds from a few centimetres to a few metres per day, but this can vary widely. At the sea, chunks of glacial ice break off into the water. This is called calving. The chunk of ice, or iceberg, floats with only one tenth of its mass above the surface, and may travel great distances. In the Antarctic, icebergs break off from the iceshelf and are often flatter, wider and more numerous than Arctic icebergs.

The tallest iceberg ever sighted was near Greenland, with almost 170 metres showing above water. The biggest iceberg was an Antarctic iceberg which covered an area the size of Belgium.

1. What is another name for 'pancake ice'? ______________________ (A short answer is required.)

2. Where are the most icebergs found? (A full-sentence answer is required.) ______________________

____

3. What fraction of an iceberg is below the water line? ______________________

4. Many of the glaciers of the Antarctic region end up as

   (A) frazel ice.   (C) pack ice.

   (B) ice floes.   (D) icebergs.

5. Select the correct fact to complete this sentence. Ships, called icebreakers, are used to

   ☐ smash icebergs. ☐ plough through pack ice. ☐ break chunks off icebergs.

6. By late summer, all Antarctic ice has melted. ☐ True ☐ False

Finding Facts—Newspaper Article: Mystery at Mandurah

by Jill Burgess

Mystery at Mandurah

In March 1969, a tragedy struck when local fishermen Hugh Gill and Bevan Hahn went fishing for crays and were never seen again.

Resident Jim Spice could recall the day he went to meet Gill's vessel, the Avaneta, at the Government jetty. But it was an appointment **she** did not keep.

Gill, 62, and Hahn, 33, were last seen shifting craypots more than 36 km off Halls Head, but an intensive search by fishermen and a coastal sweep by a **flotilla** of yachts returning from Bunbury failed to turn up any clues.

The weather was rough and the 22-year-old boat, previously wrecked on the entrance bar, should not have been rebuilt and certainly not have put to sea in the condition it was in.

Later, fisherman Ray Brennan discovered a number of craypots, floats and ropes adrift in the general area of the Avaneta's last sighting.

The floats were clearly marked with the vessel's number and an echo sounder revealed an object the size of the missing vessel 40 m down on the ocean bed.

Convinced it was the Avaneta, Brennan and others marked the spot and spent precious time needed to prepare for the crayfish season guiding police and divers to the spot.

But the search was called off when police claimed their divers were not equipped to do deep dives.

Later in the year, a row was brewing as fishermen and residents claimed police were reluctant to follow a lead which could solve the disappearance.

There were conflicting opinions as to why specialist help was not obtained and the site investigated further.

According to reports, the marker flag was moved when the dive was abandoned and the spot could not later be identified.

A second theory blamed the recent Meekering earthquake which caused tremors which set the flag adrift and shifted the vessel on the ocean bed.

The marker was eventually found miles away.

Although air, sea and land searches revealed few answers, fishermen were on the lookout for several weeks.

But the only clue ever to come to light was Gill's fishing box, found on the beach.

The Avaneta had a small cabin and craypots were stacked in the stern.

Jim Spice believed an unexpected wave could have struck the Avaneta, tossing the stern into the air and sending the craypots sliding down the deck to lodge against the cabin door.

Had the two men been in the cabin at the time, they would have been trapped as the boat capsized or was swamped.

Others maintain the Avaneta may have been swamped by a huge wave and gone to the bottom.

Whatever happened to the Avaneta and her crew is a mystery unlikely ever to be solved.

1. If Ray Brennan hadn't been assisting police he would have been ______________________________

____.

2. In the third sentence the word *she* refers to ______________________________.

3. Jim Spice believes the loss of the Avaneta was the result of

(A) rough weather.
(B) the Meekering earthquake.
(C) poor repairs to the damaged vessel after it was wrecked.
(D) an unexpected wave swamping the boat.

4. On information provided in the report, what would you conclude happened to the Avaneta?

____

5. In the report a *flotilla* is a

(A) sea patrol. (B) small fleet. (C) commander. (D) naval force.

6. Why did the residents of Mandurah become upset with the police? ______________________________

____

Finding Facts—The Tree of Life

If there is one thing that really comes to mind when the words 'South Pacific' are spoken then it must be palms, especially coconut palms. We all have images of tall coconut palms leaning gracefully over sandy coral beaches. But the coconut tree is more than a beautiful palm that is the central feature of picture postcards purchased by tourists.

To people of the South Pacific the coconut tree is also known as the 'Tree of Life'. It owes this name to the wide variety of products which the coconut palm provides from its various parts. From the leaves down to its roots it plays a significant part in the life of many island people. Name it, the coconut provides it—food, shelter or fuel—as well as income from exports.

Leaves. Coconut leaves produce good quality paper pulp, midrib brooms, hats and mats, fruit trays, wastebaskets, placemats and bags.
Coconuts (fruit). Flesh and water (often called the milk) from the young, green coconut can be taken as a health food and drink. It is also used as a main ingredient for salads and other delicacies.
Husks. Coconut husks contain 10% bristle fibre, 20% mattress filling and 70% coir. Often the husk is thrown away, but it can be used to produce a wide variety of useful products such as ropes, mats, fishing nets, household walling and floor coverings.
Water. Coconut water can be used in the production of vinegar and wine and is also used to treat a number of medical disorders.
Flesh. The white coconut flesh is a good source of protein, coconut oil, coconut flour, shredded coconut, coconut chips, and feed for animals.
Coconut shell. From the shell is made attractive handicrafts, novelty items, charcoal briquettes for cooking and high quality industrial carbons.
Trunk. The trunk of the coconut tree is a hardy and **durable** wood. It is used to make furniture. Paper pulp can also be made from the trunk.
Roots. Medicines, beverage extracts and dyes are obtained from the roots.

The English oak, the Lebanon cedar or the Australian gum tree all have a place in history but the coconut palm is the only true 'Tree of Life'.

1. What are the four useful parts of the fruit of the coconut palm?

(a) ____________ (b) ____________ (c) ____________ (d) ____________

2. How do tourists react to coconut palms? ______________________________

3. Why do many South Pacific people call the coconut palm the Tree of Life?

____

____

Basket

Fresh coconut

Coconut oil

Mosquito coil

Handicraft

Answer **true or false** to the facts expressed in Questions 4–6.

4. Medicines can be produced from the leaves. ______________

5. The wood of the coconut palm has limited use in building. ______________

6. Palm leaves can be used in paper making. ______________

7. In your own words, explain the meaning of the word *durable*. ______________________________

____

8. The South Pacific people regard the coconut palm as (Tick one box.)

☐ a visual pollution of coral beaches. ☐ a tree that is in oversupply.

☐ a tree of little local importance. ☐ one of the world's great trees.

Soap

Flooring

9. In your opinion, what part of the coconut palm is most useful?

Finding Facts—The Tommy Tycho Story

by Tommy Tycho

Since I was born, I have been surrounded by music. Not just any music, but the right kind of music.

It may seem odd to say that, but hearing good music played well by a big ensemble is something that a lot of people no longer experience or appreciate. Most people are **musically illiterate** simply because they have never been exposed to good music. Many people are unfamiliar with the sound of a symphony orchestra, which to me is the biggest instrument in the world. They hear orchestra music underscoring ads and films, they hear a trio and think of it as a band. To hear a full symphony orchestra on stage and to feel the power of the sound—it is like a tidal wave. It is an amazing experience and it is one that I was lucky enough to grow up with.

My mother was a **celebrated** soprano. Her name was Helen Tehel. She had been a member of the Vienna State Opera and the Budapest State Opera before her marriage and as a baby I was dragged along to concerts, the opera and operetta stages. I was spoilt rotten from the word go, surrounded not necessarily by classical music but good, high-quality music played well.

My mother was the sixteenth child in her family. She was the youngest and by the time she was born, her oldest sister also had a child with whom she shared a crib.

Because I lost my father when I was very young, I do not remember much about him. What I do know is largely what I have been told by my mother. I resemble him in many ways. He was evidently a very serious man, bordering on melancholy. I seem to have inherited something of that from him. Fortunately I inherited far more of my mother's vitality and energy—a real show business personality.

1. This type of writing could best be described as ______________________________.

2. A person who is *musically illiterate* would, most likely, be a person who
- (A) cannot play any musical instrument.
- (B) has inherited their ability from their parents.
- (C) has had only a limited variety of musical experiences.
- (D) has never been to a performance of a symphony orchestra.

3. Titles guide the reader to important facts. Another good title for this extract would be
- (A) Growing Up with Music.
- (B) An Amazing Experience.
- (C) Life in a Large Family.
- (D) Following in My Father's Footsteps.

4. Tommy Tycho's mother was very indulgent of him. ☐ True ☐ False

5. Full orchestras are usually used to provide music for ads. ☐ True ☐ False

6. How do you think Tommy Tycho would describe his childhood?

7. In the extract, the word *celebrated* means

☐ 'thrilling'. ☐ 'distinguished'. ☐ 'remarkable'. ☐ 'honoured'.

8. From this extract, how would you predict Tommy Tycho's life turned out?

____

9. Where do you think Tommy Tycho was born? ______________________________

Finding Facts—Fictional Writing: Night of the Muttonbirds

The story *Night of the Muttonbirds* by Mary Small is an example of **realistic writing**. It is based upon her **real-life experiences** so it is a good book for 'finding facts' that are not from factual writing.

Night of the Muttonbirds

Matthew shifted restlessly in his chair and glanced up at the schoolroom clock on the wall opposite. Ten-thirty already! What had happened? Had something gone wrong? Today was mail day but the plane was later than usual, and on this of all days when his grandmother, Annie, was returning from hospital in Tasmania. In nervous anticipation he sat staring out of the window, chewing his fingernails, listening, waiting.

"Matthew!" Mr Trent's voice was sharp. It was difficult to keep this eleven-year-old occupied in such a small class of children—all of different ages.

Matthew glanced at him in exasperation, sighed and made a half-hearted attempt to concentrate on the subject in front of him. Then, to his enormous relief, he heard it, at first indistinct but unmistakable. The low steady drone of an aircraft approaching. He stood up pushing his books aside.

"Matthew! Sit down!"

"It's coming," said Matthew. "The plane, I mean. Mr Greg's coming."

All the children sitting around the long table in the school classroom looked up.

Matthew was already halfway to the open door, his face anxious.

"Can I come too?" asked Shelley, his nine-year-old sister.

"And me too?" piped up his brother, five-year-old Clinton, his green smock splattered with bright colours from the dripping paint pots on his painting easel.

Deborah stood up. "I want to see Grannie," she said.

"And me!" cried Jim, sliding backwards off his chair.

"Sit down!" said Mr Trent crossly. "No, not you, Matthew. I promised you could come but remember it's on the condition you work through your lunch hour." With almost half the class grandchildren of old Annie, he had to be strict. "Shelley, are you listening? I'm leaving you in charge. There'll be no fooling around while I'm away."

1. Name the main character in the extract. ______________________

2. What was Shelley's relationship to Clinton? Clinton was

☐ an older sister. ☐ a younger sister. ☐ a younger brother. ☐ the only brother.

3. What was causing Matthew to be nervous?

☐ The late arrival of the plane. ☐ The return of his grandmother.

☐ Leaving Shelley in charge of the class. ☐ Not being able to finish his work on time.

4. Which word would best describe Mr Trent's behaviour as the plane approached? (Circle one.)

fearful relaxed agitated pleased distraught

5. Mr Trent found his class difficult to control because

(A) Matthew wouldn't listen. (B) the students were all different ages.

(C) the school was so small. (D) Annie was returning to Tasmania.

6. Shelley has to pick up the paint from the floor. ☐ True ☐ False

7. Mr Greg was most likely to be ______________________.

8. Who spoke the words, "Matthew! Sit down!"? ______________________

Finding Facts—Our Neighbour in Space

from the Malin Space Mission website

Mars is famous for its colour, its volcanoes and its sand dunes. Its polar regions are also of interest to scientists. The Mars Global Surveyor orbited Mars and photographed and sent back information to Earth on the North Pole of Mars.

The northern spring in Mars begins in mid July. With the arrival of spring there is the annual shrinkage of the northern polar ice cap. When sunlight begins to shine on the northern ice cap the frost and ice begin their retreat.

But this is not the normal Earth-like ice and snow that melts to become water. Mars' ice and snow is formed from carbon dioxide and when it melts it doesn't turn into a liquid—it goes directly from a solid to a gas. And when this happens the surface of Mars is quickly revealed.

What was photographed in July 1998 was a view of the Martian sand dunes. Just a few months earlier they were obscured by frost, thick cloud and the Martian night—a bit like the night at the Earth's Poles.

This vast sea of sand dunes surrounds the North Pole. They were first seen by Viking 2 Orbiter in 1976. The size and shape of the crescent dunes are similar to sand dunes found in many desert regions on Earth which are formed when the wind persistently comes from the one direction.

As spring progresses, the sky above the Martian dunes clears. Northern summers begin early in January.

Because it was in polar orbit, Mars Global Orbiter had many opportunities to photograph the region and collect important information on the changes that take place over a number of Martian seasons.

1. What is this extract about? The extract ____

____.

2. Write letters (A, B, or C) in the brackets to match the correct sentence beginnings.

(A) With the advent of spring	( ) sunlight begins to shine on the ice cap.
(B) By late January	( ) sand dunes are concealed under a frost cover.
(C) Before July	( ) the ice cap has shrunk.

3. The photographs of Mars were taken by a passing spacecraft. ☐ True ☐ False

4. The North Pole of Mars is surrounded by a vast ocean. ☐ True ☐ False

5. How does the snow and ice on Mars differ from snow and ice on Earth? ______________________

____

6. Why are the Martian sand dunes crescent shaped? ______________________________

____

7. The Mars Global Orbiter's mission was to
(A) take photos of the northern polar ice cap only.
(B) collect information about the seasons on Mars.
(C) gather samples from the Martian sand dunes.
(D) find landing sites for a scientific mission.

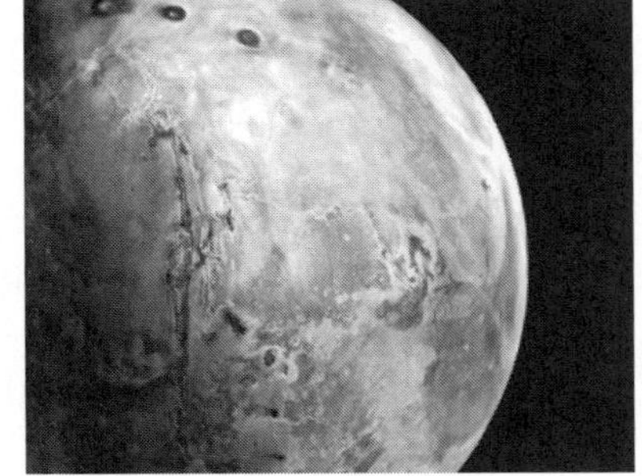

Finding the Main Idea—Native Animals as Pets

When studying texts you will often be asked to find the **main idea**. In paragraphs, the main idea is often the same as the **topic sentence**. It is the most important piece of information for the reader. All other sentences in the paragraph add to the meaning of the topic sentence. They are often called the **supporting detail** (see Understanding Paragraphs, p. 39).

The topic sentence is often the first sentence but it can come in the middle of the paragraph or at the end. If it is quite long, it may sometimes contain more information than just the main idea.

In longer works we often talk about the **theme**, or central idea. Titles and headings often give a clue about the main idea in books or in chapters. If we look at the extract 'Native Animals as Pets' from *Pets, the Law and You in NSW*, by Karen Don, we can use it to start 'finding the main idea'.

Native Animals as Pets

Pets play an important role in our society (*main idea/topic sentence*). They provide us with companionship, love and affection, benefits to our health, and sometimes even security (*supporting detail*). In order to care for our pets in the best way possible, it is important to know about the laws affecting us and our animals (*supporting detail*) …

The *National Parks and Wildlife Act 1974* contains regulations about the keeping of native animals as pets. Under the act it is an offence to buy, sell or possess protected fauna unless you have the appropriate licence. The penalty is $2000 or imprisonment for six months.

It is possible to obtain a licence from the National Parks and Wildlife Service to keep native birds and some species of reptiles. The department will only give licences for the keeping of two types of mammals—the spinifex hopping mouse and the plains rat—and will not give licences to keep native amphibians.

The penalty for keeping endangered fauna is a fine of $4000 or imprisonment for 12 months. The penalty for keeping marine mammals and threatened native fauna is a $10 000 fine or imprisonment for two years. As the regulations are constantly changing, before contemplating obtaining any sort of native animal, first check with the Service. Humane Society International does not encourage the keeping of any native animals as pets.

If you find an injured native animal or bird contact the Wildlife Information and Rescue Service (WIRES). WIRES has experienced people to nurse sick and injured animals back to health. These carers have special licences which allow them to care for animals that are otherwise illegal to keep.

1. The main idea, in the second paragraph ('The *National Parks* …'), centres on
   (A) buying and selling protected fauna.
   (B) the fines for keeping native animals.
   (C) the provisions of the *National Parks and Wildlife Act 1974*.
   (D) why people should get a licence to keep native animals.

2. What is the 'main idea' in the third paragraph?
   (A) keeping amphibians (B) two special Australian mammals
   (C) rules for keeping birds (D) obtaining licences

3. It is important for anyone who finds an injured native animal to nurse it back to health.
   ☐ True ☐ False

4. Which one of the following is a good alternative heading for this extract? (Circle one answer.)
   People Need Pets Native Fauna Regulations Saving Our Wildlife

5. What theme is developed in the text? ____________________

Finding the Main Idea—Earth First

by David Bowden and Jenny Dibley

Technology vs the environment

In Australia and other developed countries, consumption is viewed as essential for economic growth. In recent decades, however, concern has grown about the increasing number of people consuming finite resources at an alarming rate.

People in developed countries consume far more resources per person than those in developing countries. The United States has only about 5 per cent of the world's population, yet consumes about 35 per cent of the world's energy. Developed countries have the power to lead the world toward environmental **consumerism** because they use the most resources.

Sophisticated packaging and storage such as refrigeration is a luxury that consumers in developed countries take for granted. In many parts of the world where refrigeration is either unavailable or too expensive, fresh food is purchased daily from open-air markets.

These markets make little impact upon the environment. They do not use energy to store food and because they mostly operate during daylight hours, no electricity is used for lighting. Packaging is mostly unnecessary, and when needed is often made from biodegradable vegetable matter.

These markets still exist in many parts of the developed world, but are an alternative form of shopping. Even in developing countries, shops are fast becoming the primary outlets for consumers.

Commercial packaging is becoming as much a part of consumption in developing countries as it is in developed countries. Plastic bags, aluminium drink cans, cardboard cartons and polystyrene hamburger containers are now swept into rubbish piles along with banana leaves which are a more traditional form of packaging. In most cases, it all ends up at the local tip and is not recycled.

Many people are starting to notice the impact of consumerism on the environment. It is affecting not only the planet, but also our health. Some scientists think that the greenhouse effect and depletion of the ozone layer have increased due to the production, use and disposal of many of the products we use.

1. What is the main idea in the first paragraph? ______________________________

____

2. The author considers packaging and refrigeration to be (luxuries necessities progress).

3. What is meant by the word *consumerism*? ______________________________

____

4. Explain the main idea of paragraph 6. ______________________________

____

5. Paragraph 5 tells us that the trend towards open-air markets in developing countries is

(increasing declining stable).

6. When did people start becoming concerned about how resources were being consumed?

____

7. What do you think is the main point of the extract? ______________________________

____

Finding the Main Idea—Fictional Writing: Land of the Rippling Gold

Read this extract from *Land of the Rippling Gold* by Una Clarke and answer the questions.

Wendy blamed herself for the accident. If she hadn't been daydreaming out of the opposite window, she might have seen the stump and yelled in time for her father to turn the wheel. There wasn't another stump or tree on the roadside for miles. Besides, it was her fault they were even there, and now her mother sat covered with blood.

Two weeks had passed since her leg was gouged by Marjorie's bike. Christmas had come and gone. The slight wound had seemed to be healing, then suddenly swelled up in a shiny painful lump, putting her mother into a fine flap. Having suffered so dreadfully with a poisoned leg herself, and fearing for her child, she had insisted on consulting the doctor in the next town that very day. Her father, reluctant to lose a day's work, argued that a good **poulticing** would fix it. Edie had flared up at that, saying his family had said the same about her leg. So both parents had begun the journey in a grumpy mood.

They were barely out of town when it happened. Wendy remembered hearing her mother complain about losing a glove and her father's grunt as he bent down to pick it up, then the shock of the impact and his unaccustomed swearing as he jammed on the brake—too late!

He had jumped straight out, anxious to see what he had done to his car, and Wendy had followed. Surprisingly though, apart from the shattered windscreen, the solid Old Liz was hardly damaged.

Then Edie, who had not moved, said quietly, "You'd better look at me!"

They had looked—and had a dreadful shock. Blood was oozing from small cuts all over her face and streaming from several deep slashes on her temple. It was dripping from her chin and splashing all over her best ruffled pink blouse and neat brown suit.

1. Write the topic sentence for the last paragraph.

2. Number these incidents in order (1–4) from least important to most important.

   ☐ Wendy's mother lost a glove. ☐ The windscreen was shattered.

   ☐ Wendy's parents had a disagreement. ☐ Edie's face was cut.

3. Who did Wendy blame for the accident?

4. The word *poulticing* has a meaning relating to:

   ☐ a dressing. ☐ an infection. ☐ an operation.

5. Which would you consider the best title for this extract?

   ☐ Shattered Windscreen ☐ The Daydreamer

   ☐ The Accident ☐ Face Wounds

6. Wendy's parents were silent because they had disagreed. ☐ True ☐ False

7. Marjorie had been hurt in a motorbike accident. ☐ True ☐ False

8. The family was going to town because of Edie's accident. ☐ True ☐ False

9. Who do you think is the main character in the extract? ______________ What are your reasons?

____

Finding the Main Idea—Poetry: Bush Medicine

Bush Medicine

when i was a little girl
many women used to come
to my grandmother to be cured
she chewed some leaves
wrapped in more leaves
then used the juice to dry out
the **bothersome** sores
the women were always quiet
and somewhat apprehensive
now the **wise men** say
that there might be something
in my grandmother's cure
and the leaves that flavoured it
i only hope that one day
they too would be sure

by Konai Helu-Thaman

1. In this poem, it is most likely the poet's intention to
   (A) teach people how to prepare bush medicines.
   (B) ridicule doctors who won't accept bush medicines.
   (C) get readers to reconsider their attitude to bush medicines.
   (D) provide information on the collection of bush medicine ingredients.

2. The writer's grandmother chewed leaves
   (A) to release the juices.
   (B) to help her concentrate.
   (C) because she was hungry.
   (D) because she liked the taste.

3. In this poem the word *bothersome* is closest in meaning to
   (A) 'painful'.
   (B) 'annoying'.
   (C) 'contagious'.
   (D) 'unpleasant'.

4. The leaves were used for
   (A) cooking food.
   (B) making baskets.
   (C) wrapping up parcels.
   (D) healing skin problems.

5. The *wise men* referred to are probably
   (A) judges.
   (B) doctors.
   (C) lawyers.
   (D) teachers.

6. The women who came to the grandmother were
   (A) wise and bothersome.
   (B) apprehensive and wise.
   (C) quiet and apprehensive.
   (D) apprehensive and bothersome.

7. In your opinion, what is the poet's attitude towards her grandmother? ______________________

____

8. What theme is developed in the poem? ______________________

____

Finding the Main Idea—Stereotypes and Work

From *That's a Job for Me!* by Ross Pearce

"Snakes are poisonous! Quick! Kill the snake!"

Many an unfortunate non-venomous snake has been killed because we do not question the truth of our preconceived notions or stereotypes. Stereotypes are fixed ideas or feelings we have about things in our world. They influence much of our thinking. Our actions are often based on the stereotypes we hold in our minds.

In the world of work, it is easy to be influenced by these fixed concepts and stereotypes. "I can't do that job; only boys do that sort of work." "I'd like to do that when I leave school but I think that's a job for women." Such ideas can greatly reduce the jobs we might think suitable for ourselves. They become like invisible chains restricting our freedom to choose from the widest range of jobs. You must wonder why people would allow themselves to be robbed of their freedom to choose.

Stereotypes sneak into our minds without us even realising it and then they become part of our way of thinking.

* "Jenny loves bandaging cuts and bruises. She's going to be a nurse when she grows up."
* "Jason loves bandaging cuts and bruises. He's going to be a doctor when he grows up."

When Jenny and Jason watch television they see that the nurses are usually women and the doctors are usually men. So little Jenny and Jason store in their minds the stereotype that girls become nurses and boys become doctors. They do not remember where the idea came from. They believe that it was what they chose freely for themselves and what they always wanted.

To understand how stereotypes sneak into our thoughts we need to be alert for clues in what people say to us and what we hear, watch and read in the media. Television can be very influential in developing these stereotypes in people's minds.

Luckily things are changing!

1. How many paragraphs in this extract? __________
2. What is the main idea in paragraph 3? ______________________________

   ____
3. The two sentences commencing with the asterisk (*) are very similar. The differences are meant to show how much we are influenced by ______________________________.
4. Which of the following statements is an example of stereotyping?
   (A) Sally Pearson is one of Australia's great hurdlers.
   (B) Men's sport is more exciting to watch than women's sport.
   (C) It is important to offer your seat to an elderly person on a bus.
   (D) Many people believe farmers should have guns to shoot feral animals.
5. How does the writer feel about stereotyping in today's society? ______________________________

   ____
6. If you had to give the extract another title, a good one would be

   ☐ Finding a Job. ☐ Doctors and Nurses. ☐ Reasons to Kill Snakes. ☐ Changing Attitudes.
7. The theme for this passage could be: Stereotyping benefits ______________________________.
8. According to the text, most people probably have some fixed ideas. ☐ True ☐ False
9. Give an example of stereotyping you have come across. ______________________________

   ____

Finding the Main Idea—The Band

Read this extract from *Perfect Timing* by Jeremy Fisher and answer the questions.

Inside the hall, streamers and balloons were in profusion. Andrew recognised the streamers and decorations he had made among the many hanging from the ceiling and walls. He was pleased that the junk material they had gathered up and recycled had turned out looking so sharp.

Gaggles of kids stood about, talking excitedly about their clothes, their hair—for some of the boys had gone for a greased-back look, and several of the girls had teased their hair into towering beehives—and, of course, the band. At the end of the hall, on a small raised platform, stood a familiar drum kit. Guitars rested on their metal stands in front of it, and a keyboard system was arranged to one side. Large speakers had been placed on either side of the platform.

Nick and Tim ran up to Andrew and Amanda.

"Andrew," Nick excitedly said, "it's fantastic! They're really here. Even after winning the awards. They've still come to play for us!"

Right then, the lights dimmed. A hush fell over the hall, and all eyes fixed on the stage.

Suddenly lights flashed and—zap!—there was the band! They began their first song to the accompaniment of great multicoloured bursts of light which swirled about them.

Once they had finished, they began another of their hits, and then another. Andrew stood transfixed as the music rolled around him. It was as if he were suspended in space somewhere, seeing and hearing everything, but invisible to all about him.

Then the band finished their **set**. The applause went on and on. Nick and Matt were whistling and stamping their feet, and shouting out their approval. Andrew, out of his spell, had yelled himself hoarse. Amanda's hands were stinging from the number of times she'd clapped them together.

1. The extract is mainly about ______________________________.

2. What word do you think could best replace *gaggles*?
   (A) groups (B) hundreds (C) an assembly (D) a collection

3. If you had to give the extract a title, a good title would be:
   ☐ Space Age Music. ☐ Another Night Out. ☐ A Stunning Act. ☐ The Decorated Hall.

4. Below is the seventh paragraph. Tick the box to show which sentence contains the main idea.
   ☐ Once they had finished, they began another of their hits, and then another.
   ☐ Andrew stood transfixed as the music rolled around him.
   ☐ It was as if he were suspended in space somewhere, seeing and hearing everything, but invisible to all about him.

5. When the audience arrived the band was already on the platform. ☐ True ☐ False

6. Amanda enjoyed the show as much as Nick. ☐ True ☐ False

7. What is the *set* that is referred to in the last paragraph? ______________________________

8. The band received (an enthusiastic an exhausting a conventional) response. (Circle one answer.)

9. Give two ways appreciation was shown for the band. ______________ ______________

What's the Inference?—Streetscape

Making an inference is a thinking or reasoning skill (see also Drawing Conclusions, p. 28). The reader is often only given a limited amount of information and makes inferences from the information given. Readers also use their general knowledge when making inferences. Read the following short passage.

> Bradley walked into the room and kicked the sleeping bag to the other side of the room. The dog, sprawled on its belly, looked up for a moment then put its head back onto its outstretched front paws.
> Bradley sniffed noisily and dropped his haversack onto the bare boards as he headed to the ancient fridge.

The reader could make several inferences from this passage. What sort of a person was Bradley? Why did he kick the sleeping bag? Why was the dog so uninterested? From the evidence, the reader could probably **infer** that Bradley was in a bad mood. Because the dog didn't react the reader might also infer that Bradley was often in a bad mood. It is likely that the room is not Bradley's usual room and that he is probably camping there. The reader might also make some **inferences** about how Bradley feels about his present situation.

Sometimes writers will deliberately mislead the reader. They do not give all the information or they add information that gives the reader the wrong ideas or impressions. This happens in mystery stories and some horror books.

Now read this extract from *Streetscape* by Ian Steep and answer the questions.

> Michael and Nicole cautiously made their way along a side lane until they were out of sight of the street and the neighbouring windows. The side fence was well protected by shrubs and vines, making it easy to get over unseen. Michael swung onto the lower branches of a big jacaranda and looked around. The leaves still covered him. Nicole perched on a branch behind him.
>
> "Go on, get moving," she hissed.
>
> **Stealthily** they crept along the branch until, stretching out, they reached the balcony. There was no movement in the house and the street was quiet. Keeping low, they picked their way between the terracotta pots and geraniums behind the balcony wall. Sliding glass doors led into the upstairs rooms. The curtains were drawn making it impossible to see inside. A thin strip of silver ran around the perimeter of the doors.
>
> "Blast!" whispered Nicole angrily. "It's alarmed."
>
> At the last set of doors, nearest the back of the house, there were no curtains, just a long venetian blind. The slats stood open. Michael and Nicole approached it cautiously. A gentle tug on the latch showed that the door was locked.

1. The reader could infer that Michael and Nicole were involved in a criminal act. Give one reason for this inference. ______________________

2. The reader can infer that Michael and Nicole may have been used to this sort of activity. What evidence suggests this? ______________________

3. How does the author create a feeling of suspense? ______________________

4. The house was probably empty. This can be best inferred from the fact that
   ☐ some curtains were closed. ☐ the balcony was scaled. ☐ the alarm was set.

5. If something is being done *stealthily*, it is done in what manner? ______________________ .

6. It is most likely that this was not the first time Michael and Nicole had seen the house. What reason could you give for this inference? ______________________

   ____

What's the Inference?—The Lady in Black

Winter.

One in the morning, Monday 9 June.

Night has leached life from the suburbs on the surrounding hills and from the wharves around the Backwater Bay. The bus is a vulnerable glow-worm of light crawling along the wet, black road.

Brett stares absentmindedly through the window glare into the damp gloom. All he can see is the pool of yellow light racing along the road as if accompanying the bus on its **silent mission**. The road could well be part of the black surface of still water of the nearby bay. The scattered lights of the city centre are lost in the cold mist that drifts across the water and seeps into the surrounding locked suburbs.

The bus stops for some T intersection lights that carry on their relentless cycle of amber, red, green though the bus is the only traffic at this hour. It could be a ghost town. Brett stares out into the bushes growing along the roadside. A sign states that the landscaping is a government project to green the environment with natural vegetation.

Behind the saplings and bushes are the vague skeletal structures of a silent railway goods yard. Brett shivers and thinks how great it will be to get into bed. Selling hamburgers on the late night shift was not a great challenge but it gave him some holiday cash.

The bus shudders gently forward as the lights change to green.

Out of the corner of his eye Brett catches sight of a movement in a gap in the shrubbery. For a moment he thinks it his reflection in the lightly misted glass. He hadn't seen the person until she moved and he almost calls out to the driver to stop then suddenly realises she probably does want to catch the bus. It isn't a regular bus stop.

1. The writer creates a special mood (or atmosphere) in this extract. In your opinion the extract best creates a mood of

(A) fear. (B) sorrow. (C) anxiety. (D) foreboding.

2. From the information in the extract, Brett could best be described as

☐ aggressive. ☐ belligerent. ☐ sombre.
☐ industrious. ☐ annoyed. ☐ meddlesome.
☐ impertinent. ☐ detached.

3. Give two words of opposite meaning that would describe the world outside the bus and the environment in the bus. (a) ______________ (b) ______________

4. In your opinion, what is the most important thing that happens in the extract?

____

5. Find three references (allusions) to death in the extract.

(a) ______________ (b) ______________ (c) ______________

6. The bus has a *silent mission*. What do you think that mission might be? ______________

____

7. Which word best describes Brett's attitude to his job? ☐ indifference ☐ dedication

What's the Inference?—Odious Underarmus, Marathon Man

by Bill Condon and Dianne Bates

CHARACTERS: **Odious Underarmus**: fishmonger, **Billious**: Odious's friend, **Jilly Achilles**: a maiden, **Regurgitus**: Jilly's handmaiden, **Achilles:** Jilly's father, **Tyrannus Dreadus**: Jilly's betrothed, **Narratus**, **the Oracle**, **a crowd**

SCENE 1: *A crowded market place in ancient Greece.*

ODIOUS: *(calling)* Salmon, snapper, sardines, stingray, shark, squid, shrimps, swordfish, sole, sturgeon, seal! Freshly caught last week! Getcha red-hot fishies. Salmon, snapper . . .

(He continues to mime as Narratus steps forward from the crowd.)

NARRATUS: Ladies and gentlemen, welcome to a typical day in the tiny Grecian village of Athos in the Year 776 BC. Behind me is a typical smelly fishmonger of these parts, Odious Underarmus, selling typically smelly fish. What Odious does not realise is that any minute now, the course of his life is going to dramatically change—in fact, what you are about to witness is the beginning of a 'wimpsical' romance.

(Jilly, Achilles and Regurgitus enter.)

REGURGITUS: Hurry along now, Jilly. You know we'll be in trouble if they find out we're from Spartica.

JILLY: Don't be so cowardly, Regurgitus; a Spartan has no fear of anything, let alone these imbecilic Athenians.

ODIOUS: Salmon, snapper, sea lion, stingray. Getcha red-hot fishies. Fish, miss? Care for some week-old fishies?

JILLY: Do you have any smoked shicklebocks?

ODIOUS: I smoked the last one yesterday.

JILLY: Well, do you have any nice eyes? *(Pause)* Why did I say nice eyes?

ODIOUS: Because you have—you have nice eyes.

REGURGITUS: Oh, oh! I've seen that look before.

NARRATUS: The look of love!

REGURGITUS: Exactly! I don't like the look of this. Hurry, Jilly! Let's go.

JILLY: *(to Odious)* I do like your looks, Mr ... Mr ...?

ODIOUS: Odious Underarmus, Miss.

REGURGITUS: This can't go any further, Jilly. Your father would never agree to you having anything to do with an Athenian.

JILLY: An oracle once told me I would **hook** the man of my dreams ...

ODIOUS: My mum always said I was a **good catch**.

1. The intended audience for a production of this play would most likely be ____________________.

2. A number of the characters' names are
   (A) names from ancient Greece.
   (B) common, modern Grecian names.
   (C) meant to give authenticity and dignity to the play.
   (D) names referring to unpleasant human functions.

3. This play could best be described as
   (A) a comedy. (B) a tragedy. (C) educational.

4. What is the importance of the words *hook* and *good catch*? ____________________

   ____

5. Make two observations about the fish Odious is selling.
   (a) ____________________ (b) ____________________

6. From the information in the extract, you would infer that Odious is
   (A) an official. (B) a buffoon. (C) an idealist. (D) a leader.

7. A person who is **betrothed** is (married promised disobedient impaired). (Circle one answer.)

What's the Inference?—Comics: Politically Correct

by Greg Anderson-Clift

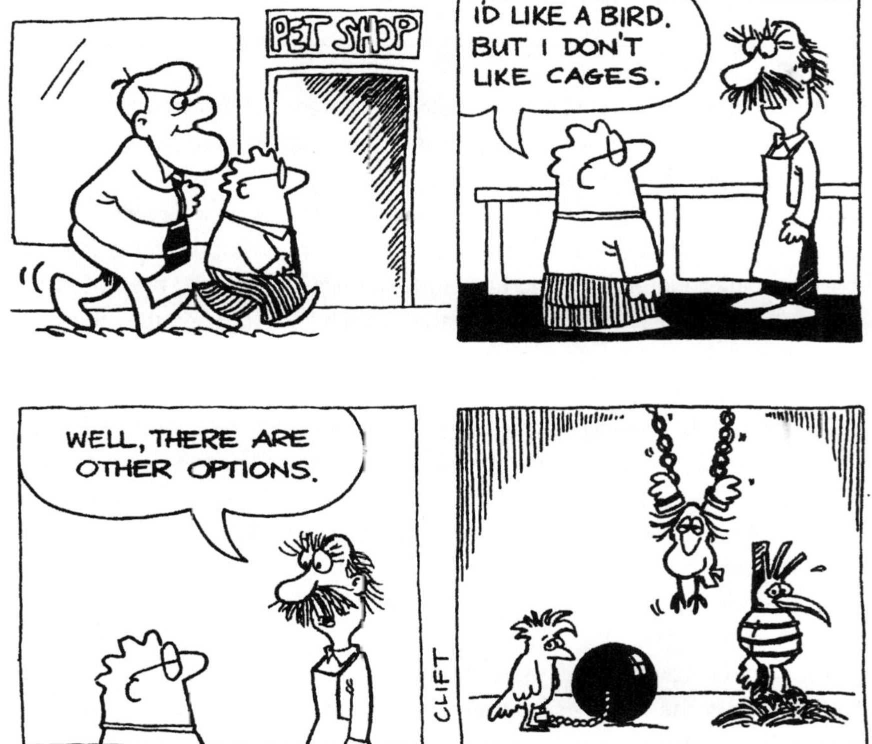

Read this short comic strip in which Max (tall) and Leon (short) visit a pet shop.

1. Humour in comics often depends upon 'misunderstandings'. In your opinion, who in this comic strip most misunderstands the situation? ____________________

2. In your opinion, are any of the comic characters stereotyped? Yes / No

   If Yes, who? ______________ How? ____________________

3. Comics often make use of facial features. What inferences can you make about the expression of the pet shop owner in frame 3? ____________________

4. Comic characters often overreact or underreact. Which character, in your opinion, would be least stressed by the situation shown in the last frame? ____________________

5. How do you think most readers would react to frame 4?
   (A) amused but upset
   (B) angry and appalled
   (C) depressed and helpless
   (D) pleased but weary

6. Comics often comment on social issues. What issue do you think is being commented upon in this comic strip? ____________________

What's the Inference?—An Interview with Victor Marshall

This is part of an interview with Victor Marshall, a television current affairs presenter. Lee Price is the interviewer. Interviews are recorded in a similar way to the dialogue of a play.

Lee Price: What do you do on TV?

Victor Marshall: I am the presenter of a current affairs program called 'Marshall's Morning'. 'Marshall's Morning' provides an analysis of what is happening in Australia and across the world.

LP: What do you do as a presenter of current affairs?

VM: You start with an introduction to reports and conduct comments on interviews. Depending on the current issues, I believe that between 60 per cent and 80 per cent of the programs is of me, or an outside reporter, doing an interview. You have to be a reliable, informed presenter. Your audience may only watch you once or twice a week, but they switch you on when they think you may have something on a topical issue that affects them.

LP: What happens if you are sick?

VM: Me? Get sick? I'm always there—fingers crossed. That way you develop a loyal audience. I was a foreign correspondent in 2008. I can contact diplomats in most countries because I have been in the field as long as most of them. I can easily include famous—or infamous—people without too much hassle.

LP: There are important personalities you can contact, which gives 'Marshall's Morning' the edge over other morning TV current affairs shows.

VM: That's about how it works. I've been part of TV reporting in Australia and overseas, so a lot of people have heard of me or have met me.

LP: What sort of contact do you have with your audience?

VM: Well, I don't do talkback the way they do on radio. But we do take a few selected twitter comments. We can't respond to them all!

LP: What sorts of issues get people going?

VM: People contact the station for many reasons. A number often want to congratulate you on a show well researched. Mainly the people who contact the station by phone or email want to complain about something. Or feel their side of an issue wasn't fairly treated. You sometimes feel like opting out of such 'debates', but **that's death professionally**. You can't do it. It's important knowing what some people think, even if you strongly disagree with what they have to say.

1. From the interview extract, Victor Marshall could best be described as
   (A) a committed presenter.
   (B) an opinionated presenter.
   (C) an intolerant presenter.
   (D) a nonchalant presenter.

2. As an interviewer, Lee Price could best be described as
   ☐ sympathetic. ☐ aggressive. ☐ forthright. ☐ persistent.

3. What does Victor Marshall mean when he says: "that's death professionally"? ____________________

   ____

4. The relationship between the interviewer and interviewee could best be described as
   ☐ cautious. ☐ tense. ☐ cordial. ☐ informal.

5. Victor Marshall's journalistic experience makes him a valued presenter. ☐ True ☐ False

6. It is likely that most people who listen to 'Marshall's Morning' ________________ (verb) Victor Marshall's presentation.

What's the Inference?—Book Review: Code of Deception

Code of Deception by Ted Ottley

This is a story of revenge. It is an electronics based, science fiction, adventure thriller. There are obvious goodies and baddies and a range of characters whose sympathies and intentions are slowly revealed. It is a story of Lear Jets, mysterious cars, bugging, drugs and corruption in high places.

Jake Carson, at fifteen, is a swimming coach and computer genius. He lives happily with his father. Unknown to him his life is under threat from the neo-Nazi Dr Mulder. Because Jake's grandfather allegedly stole the plans for the **prototype** of an electronic games industry from the doctor, Jake and his father become the focus of the doctor's **unrelenting revenge obsession**. Mulder has destroyed the family company and is bent on destroying the Carson family. He uses his twisted brilliance to develop a virtual reality computer game that can also simulate emotions—**virtual emotions**—which were obtained through the use of real encounters with death.

Ted Ottley's journalistic style is pacy with sudden breaks and moves. The story is compact and of the moment, even though it weaves a web of intrigue across three generations and along the eastern seaboard of Australia. There are no loose ends. The climax is frightening and the epilogue is sinister and is an obvious opening for a sequel.

The story raises obvious moral questions, not only about the ethics of company espionage, but just where the ever increasing pace of technological change is leading the world. Do we still have control over our own lives?

from *Magpies Magazine*

1. From the points made in the review, a reader could infer that the reviewer
   (A) was receptive to the book's style.
   (B) found the book lacked credibility.
   (C) found little to recommend the book.
   (D) was critical of the book's subject matter.

2. The review was most likely written for the benefit of

   ☐ the author. ☐ the publisher. ☐ journalists. ☐ librarians.

3. A *prototype* is
   (A) the first model successfully tested.
   (B) a standard production model.
   (C) one of the first models tested.
   (D) one in a series of commercial models.

4. Why does the character Dr Mulder want to take revenge on Jake and his father? ____________________

   ____

5. Referring to the text, what word would you use to describe Dr Mulder? ____________________

6. A person who has an *unrelenting revenge obsession* could be described as

   (consumed by hate   paralysed by delusion   goaded by fear). (Circle one answer.)

7. Would the book appeal to you? _____ Why? ____________________

8. Use the numbers 1, 2 and 3 to sequence the order in which events happened (from first to last).

   ☐ Carson's family company is destroyed.
   ☐ The plans for an electronic game are stolen.
   ☐ At fifteen, Jake is a computer genius and swimming coach.

9. How are *virtual emotions* obtained? ____________________

Using Context Clues—The Incredible Experience of Megan Kingsley

Sometimes when we read we are not always directly told all the information. Often we can work out what is happening, how people feel or where the action is from information in the writing. The context can also give clues to the meaning of new or unusual words.

Read this short passage from *Circles* by William Taylor.

> Today I pushed my way through the undergrowth, doing my best to follow the ill-formed track to the spot beneath the giant rimu tree where a slab of marble says: Elizabeth Costello 1840–1876 and John Costello 1839–1876. My father, foolish man, lost spirit, survived his wife by no more than a handful of hours. Robert and I dug his grave and then we left this place with, in reality, little hope of ever seeing it again.

From the text we get clues about what might be going on: something sorrowful seems to be taking place (the narrator is visiting his parents' graves in some neglected place). There is also a sense of loneliness (the narrator is alone in an isolated bush environment). We get this information from the **context** in which it appears. We use **context clues**.

Read this extract from *The Incredible Experience of Megan Kingsley* by Pamela O'Connor and answer the questions.

> A loud scraping noise sent her to the window again. The loose sheet of corrugated iron was being blown across the ground. Rain had not yet begun to fall, but the clouds were so low and menacing that Megan shivered as she sat and watched them. What a horrible, swirling black nightmare was out there!
>
> She backed away from the window. The strange stabbing feeling in her stomach became worse and she lay down on her bed, knees drawn up under her chin, wondering what terrible disaster was going to overtake them. She tried to tell herself she was being foolish, but the feeling would not go away.
>
> Megan felt a tugging at her arm and Annabel climbed in next to her. "I don't like the storm, Megan. I'm frightened."
>
> Megan hugged her.
>
> "Is the island going to blow away?"
>
> "No, of course not."
>
> "Are you sure the cubby will still be all right?"
>
> "I'm sure." A small lie wouldn't hurt.
>
> "D'you think Aurora's frightened of storms?"
>
> "She probably is. She's the same as you and me."
>
> "No, she isn't." Annabel's voice was **muffled** against Megan's shoulder. "She's special."
>
> Megan said nothing. What was there to say?
>
> When Mrs Kingsley came in later to see why everyone was so quiet, she found them all in Megan's bed. All sound asleep—Annabel in Megan's arms and Patrick curled up like a puppy at the end of the bed.

1. The storm that Megan saw out the window
   (A) was pelting the house. (B) was approaching. (C) had passed. (D) was spent.
2. Why do you think Megan told a lie to Annabel? ______________________________
   ____
3. Why was Annabel's voice *muffled*? __________________________________
4. What do you think caused the pain in Megan's stomach? ________________________
5. Megan could best be described as being selfish. ☐ True ☐ False
6. About how old do you think Annabel was? _____ Why? (briefly) ____________________
7. What reason can you suggest for Megan NOT replying to Annabel? ____________________
   ____

Using Context Clues—The Second Plane

Aaron looked out the small window. Great sun-drenched islands of rounded clouds stretched to the horizon. The scene hadn't changed much in the last thirty minutes.

Through breaks in the clouds he caught fleeting glimpses of the azure ocean below.

Aaron was about to look back to his book when he caught sight of another plane disappearing behind a small bank of billowing clouds. He hadn't really expected to see another plane in this part of the world. A fleeting moment of uneasiness shadowed his travel-weary mind.

When the plane emerged from behind the clouds he guessed it was quite large even though it was still a long way off. It was certainly much larger than the inter-island Bandierante he was on.

There was a brief moment of turbulence. Unconsciously Aaron tapped the ventilator he carried in his denim jacket.

The new plane was turning, starting to descend in a huge arc.

A vague sense of apprehension furrowed Aaron's brow.

Aaron touched his mother's elbow. She looked up and smiled as he pointed through the round window. His mother leaned across and peered out across the clouds.

After a moment she looked at him inquiringly. "What was it?" She spoke slowly, mouthing the words over the roar of the twin engines.

Aaron took a quick look but the plane had disappeared. He shrugged his shoulders and forced a smile.

His mother copied his actions and returned to her leaflet of Autitaki's tourist attractions.

Aaron looked out the window. The lonely sky seemed to go on forever. The deserted ocean appeared endless. He resisted the urge to tap his puffer and returned to his book his father had insisted he take on holidays. But he was **reading the words and not connecting with the story**.

Absentmindedly he looked out the window. To his amazement the other plane was just emerging from a mass of misty cloud. For a brief, heart-stopping moment he thought the planes might collide. He quickly realised that it was passing right under the little Air Rarotonga Bandierante. Its details were clear.

1. Name two actions that suggest Aaron was troubled.
(a) ______________________ (b) ______________________

2. Aaron arrived at the Cook Islands on a
☐ 747 jet. ☐ Bandierante. ☐ four-engine, propeller-driven plane.

3. Give one word to describe how Aaron's mother was feeling during the trip. ______________

4. Explain your choice. ______________________

5. Aaron's mother was preoccupied with:
(air safety holiday plans Aaron's medication weather conditions). (Circle one answer.)

6. The phrase *reading the words and not connecting with the story* suggests that Aaron
☐ couldn't understand the story. ☐ found the words too difficult to read.
☐ kept losing his place on the page. ☐ was reading without thinking about the meaning.

7. Aaron tapped his ventilator out of habit. ☐ True ☐ False

8. Aaron's father had insisted that Aaron take a book on holidays. ☐ True ☐ False

9. This is the start of a story. The writing style indicates it will most likely be a/an ____________ story.

Using Context Clues—Special Day

There was one special day I remember,
when the sun set fire to the sky,
and I was at the blue-rimmed beach,
and I ran skidding down the steep green hill
to the silver-glinting shore.
The white-topped waves swung skywards
recklessly,
maybe trying to put out the fire in the sky.
I thrust myself at the ocean,
snatching for action
not wanting to waste one greedy moment,
not wanting to miss one searching wave.
It was a good day, that special day,
it had a good beginning
and no real ending:
there were no clocks out there
where the waves **wallowed** on the sand:
no trannies screamed out the seconds
and the minutes
and the hours . . .
Eventually, I suppose, the day ended,
and the night must have swallowed up the fire,
and I must have plodded up the green hill
sometime.
Days have passed since then,
Days without number.
Days and nights; time;
oceans of time.
Yet that one day, that special day,
clings on to me forever,
with the sun setting fire to the sky
and the sand on the shore glinting silver
and the white topped waves reaching out for
me …

by David Bateson (1977)

1. The special day was a day spent
(A) surfing. (B) climbing hills. (C) writing poetry. (D) listening to the trannie.

2. This poem was most likely written
(A) during the time on the beach. (C) when the poet had returned home.
(B) before skidding down the green hill. (D) a long time after the actual event.

3. For the poet, the special day could be best described as
(A) memorable. (B) traditional. (C) typical. (D) ordinary.

4. The lines: no trannies screamed out the seconds
and the minutes
and the hours … are most likely intended to show how
(A) lonely the poet was. (C) much fun the poet was having.
(B) time did not matter to the poet. (D) the poet kept a check on time.

5. The poem creates a feeling of
(A) regret. (B) sorrow. (C) hope. (D) nostalgia.

6. The word *wallowed* means to
(A) roll about. (B) crash down. (C) sweep over. (D) tumble into.

7. How did the poet feel after his special day?
(A) contented (B) melancholy (C) depressed (D) excited

8. In your opinion, how old was the poet on the special day? about ________

9. What information in the poem supports your conclusion? ______________________________

Using Context Clues—Rugby Union

from *Sport in the Making* by Shane Power

The game of **Rugby** Union began in the middle of a traditional English soccer game in 1823. William Webb Ellis was a student at the famous Rugby School in England. He was playing in an interclass match when he suddenly felt like picking the ball up. He did just that and raced off to the other end of the field with the ball tucked under his arm. Players and spectators were astonished. This action was against the rules and caused Ellis's team to look foolish. It did not take long for the news of the incident to spread to other schools. Football enthusiasts were talking about it and arguing for and against the handling of the ball.

Some players liked the idea of running with the ball so much that they introduced this new rule into the game. The students at Cambridge University were among those who were 'having a go at the game of Rugby'. At first, a player could only run with the ball if it was a fair catch. It took many years for this game to be accepted by schools and clubs. Rugby College itself did not play the new rule until 18 years after the Ellis incident.

By 1848, so many schools had introduced the rule that a meeting was called to draw up a common list of rules for everyone to follow. At this stage, the game was only played in schools and universities. It was called Rugby, or Rugger, after the school where Ellis performed his feat.

By 1872, 21 clubs had formed an amateur organisation which they called Rugby Union. No professional footballers were allowed to play the game. Each team fielded 20 players but this was later reduced to 15 a side, the same as today's teams.

The first international Rugby match was played between England and Scotland in the same year that Rugby Union was formed. The Scottish team won that historic match. It was only a matter of time before the game had spread far and wide to other parts of the world, including France, the United States, New Zealand and Africa.

1. Richard Ellis's action could best be described as
   ☐ predictable. ☐ preventable. ☐ impetuous. ☐ hazardous.

2. In your opinion, why did it take Rugby many years to catch on? ____________________

   ____

3. In your opinion, why was the first international Rugby match played against Scotland?
   (A) The Scottish people didn't play soccer.
   (B) Scotland is just across a land border from England.
   (C) The Scots had been playing Rugby longer than the English.
   (D) There were no professional football players in Scotland.

4. Number the boxes (1–4) to show the sequence in which events happened.
   ☐ The students at Cambridge begin playing Rugby.
   ☐ Ellis disrupts a soccer match by picking up the ball.
   ☐ An organisation called Rugby Union is formed.
   ☐ Rugby School introduces the game of Rugby.

5. Why was the new game called *Rugby*? Give your reason. ____________________

   ____

6. It was a while before Rugby was played outside school situations. ☐ True ☐ False

Drawing Conclusions— Warbirds over Wanaka

Drawing conclusions is an advanced reading skill. It requires you to make a judgement about what you have read. It may involve finding the main idea (p. 12), making inferences (p. 18) and using context clues (p. 24). It is related to other reading skills such as recognising fact and opinion (p. 46) and being able to distinguish between relevant and irrelevant information (p. 50).

A conclusion is reached by reasoning (thinking about a situation). You may be required to have an opinion or make a decision. You may have to justify your opinion or reason. Drawing conclusions can only be done after you have read the whole extract (or story)—when you have all the information.

Read the article 'Warbirds over Wanaka' by Shiri Gounder and answer the questions.

Wanaka is a scenic little town about 80 km north-west of Queenstown in New Zealand. It stays fairly dry and sunny, and despite the snow-capped peaks in the distance, temperatures remain mild. Wanaka is popular with tourists and seems to have a disproportionate number of hotels and motels.

Every two years, though, over the long Easter weekend, Wanaka's normal influx of visitors positively explodes; 75 000 people drawn by a three-day air show billed as 'Warbirds over Wanaka'.

Aviation buffs make up most of the crowd, but the display of ex-military vehicles, vintage motorcycles, farm machinery and antique fire engines has a certain appeal as well.

On the ground the vintage aircraft look spectacular. In the air, they're even more awesome, with aerial flying and stunt displays performed by the RNZAF Red Checkers and the Roaring Forties Harvard aerobatic teams.

In the 1998 Easter show, the war birds had a predominantly Russian theme—five Polikarpov I-16s of the Alpine Fighter Collection (the only ones flying in the world); a Russian Sukhoi Su-31, flown by Australian aerobatic champion Nigel Arnot; and a MiG-15, which flew a mock dogfight against a similar vintage P51 Mustang. Even a Catalina flying boat, a PBY which should be familiar to Kiwis, had a red star on its tail.

It was a rich assortment of aircraft, military and otherwise: stunt planes like the Boeing Stearman and Tiger Moth; training planes like the Harvards; warbirds like Corsairs, Spitfires and Mustangs … the planes that made history and, in some cases, turned the tide of world events.

And there is still time to book one of those Wanaka motels for the next big show.

1. The writer finds the air show at Wanaka
   (A) provincial. (B) excessive. (C) wondrous. (D) predictable.

2. What information leads you to the conclusion that the organiser of the air show did a good job?

   ____

3. Most of the time, Wanaka could be described as (peaceful distinguished exciting). (Circle one answer.)

4. A good title for the extract would be ☐ Wanaka Warplanes. ☐ Hotels of Wanaka.

5. What information leads you to the conclusion that the show is not just for air enthusiasts?

   ____

6. Most of the year, there is little to attract tourists to Wanaka. ☐ True ☐ False

7. The people of Wanaka would find that the article paints
   (an idealistic a sentimental a positive a dubious) picture of their town. (Circle one answer.)

Drawing Conclusions—Recipes: Puddings

from *Roland Harvey's Book of Christmas* by Roland Harvey

The exercises on this page are based upon recipes for Australian puddings.

Billy Can Pudding

1½ cups raisins
1 cup sugar
½ teaspoon mixed spice and cinnamon
2 cups plain flour
1 teaspoon bicarb. soda

Combine all ingredients. Mix well with 500 ml of boiling tea. Empty into greased and **floured** billy can. Cover. Stand overnight. Steam 3½ hours.

The Drover's Plum Pudding

250 g rice
sweetened water
sugar
125 g raisins or sultanas
handful of nuts

Put rice in saucepan or billy can of boiling, sweetened water and simmer until no water is left. Add remaining ingredients. Sweeten to taste.

1. These recipes are most likely meant for a
(A) family on a camping holiday.
(B) chef in a restaurant.
(C) meal at home.
(D) birthday party.

2. What conclusions do you draw about the origins of these recipes? ______________________________

____

3. Which of these statements is true?
(A) Both puddings must be cooked in an oven.
(B) The Billy Can Pudding is mixed with water.
(C) It takes 3½ hours to make the Drover's Plum Pudding.
(D) The Billy Can Pudding needs raisins, mixed spice and cinnamon.

4. A *floured* billy can would
(A) be rolled in flour.
(B) have roses painted on it.
(C) be dusted inside with flour.
(D) have a brand of flour stamped on it.

5. To make the Drover's Plum Pudding you would need
(A) rice, sugar, sultanas, nuts.
(B) sultanas, spice, cinnamon, nuts.
(C) cinnamon, rice, sultanas, currants.
(D) rice, mixed spice, raisins, sultanas.

6. What features do most of the ingredients in these recipes have in common?

____

____

7. After studying these recipes, a reader would conclude they came from a book about
(A) caring for sheep.
(B) cooking for a family.
(C) the Australian outback.
(D) growing your own food.

8. What word would you use to describe the cost of preparing these puddings? ____________________

9. Which pudding takes the longest time to prepare? ______________________________

Drawing Conclusions—Tsunami

tsunami (soo nah me) noun, series of long, high sea waves caused by a disturbance of ocean floor or seismic movement. [Jap. *tsu* harbour, *nami* wave]
A tsunami is not a tidal wave. It has nothing to do with tides. Tsunamis can be caused by earthquakes, volcanic action on the ocean floor, volcanoes dumping huge amounts of material into the ocean and coastal and marine landslides. Large meteors plunging into the ocean may also cause tsunamis.

1883: Java and Sumatra
The largest tsunami in historical times was generated by the eruption of Krakatoa volcano in 1883. The island that was Krakatoa was literally blown apart. The tsunami generated impacted on the nearby islands of Java and Sumatra, at a breaking height of an estimated 40 m. Approximately 36 000 people were drowned.

1946: Hawaii and California
In 1946 a magnitude 7.2 on the Richter Scale submarine earthquake occurred near Unimak Island, Alaska, and it was about five hours later the tsunamis hit the Hawaiian Islands. The wave, less than one metre in height in the open ocean, raced across the Pacific Ocean at speeds of about 800 km/hr and as it encountered the shallow waters in Hilo Harbour, over 5000 kilometres away, it rose to a breaking wave of some 18 metres high. It demolished 500 homes and killed 159 people. It also impacted on the Californian coast where it killed several people.

Today the Tsunamis Warning System in Hawaii keeps a round-the-clock **vigil** using computers and satellites. If a tsunami is confirmed, warnings are transmitted to all potentially threatened points in the Pacific.

1998: Papua New Guinea
The recent tsunami in Papua New Guinea resulted from a shallow underwater earthquake, 30 kilometres off the north coast, generating a succession of three waves rising to heights of 10 metres. Three villages, Arop, Nimas and Waropu, were completely destroyed while others received extensive damage. The three devastated villages had a population of 8000 inhabitants and approximately 2200 people died. Reports indicate that it was mostly the elderly and children who were killed in the disaster.

The tsunami was totally unexpected and no warning system would have helped, due to the close proximity to the earthquake centre.

1. Which event is the least likely to be the cause of a tsunami?
(A) an earthquake (C) a falling meteor
(B) a landslide (D) a volcanic explosion

2. From the information it can be concluded that tsunamis are rare events. ☐ True ☐ False

3. Tsunamis are most dangerous when they (Tick two boxes.)
☐ reach shallow water. ☐ have their origins close to the shore.
☐ turn into tidal waves. ☐ are recorded on the Tsunami Warning System.

4. A *vigil* is a form of (keeping watch judgement record protection). (Circle one answer.)

5. A warning system could have saved lives in Papua New Guinea. ☐ True ☐ False

6. The word *tsunami* is of ____________________ origin.

7. The 1883 tsunami was caused by a ____________________________ and the 1946 tsunami was caused by an ____________________________________ .

8. Which of the above disasters caused the greatest loss of life? ______________________________

9. It could be concluded that a reading of 7.2 on the Richter Scale is a (high low) reading. (Circle one answer.)

Drawing Conclusions—Fiction: The Tattooed Man

Mel stared at the black panther across the silver bar. It was shiny and sleek and its eyes seemed to glint as it gently rolled its lithe muscles.

He could almost see the claws.

The bus pitched into the bus stop. The doors pulled open and there was a jostle as people pressed towards the exit, eager to get off but reluctant to face the damp night air.

Mel turned to the wet, exhausted street, choked with sodden traffic. It was early evening and the neons from the shops were making shimmering splashes of lurid colour across the shiny, black surface of the road. Black like the coat of the panther. Shimmering like the panther's eyes.

The bus pulled back into the stream of traffic.

Mel turned back to the panther. With each movement of the man's shoulder it seemed to come to life, gently flexing. Its torso seemed to swell and subside and it appeared to be climbing up the man's shoulder muscle as he turned the pages in the magazine he was reading.

The bus came to a sudden halt. Some fool had dashed through the slow moving traffic. There was a red burst of tail lights. In the bus, standing passengers lurched forward, grabbing for rails and the backs of seats. Several horns blasted before the pedestrian hit the other side of the wide street—pretending to be oblivious of the trauma he had just created. Then he was lost in the damp, clammy crowd.

The tattooed man looked around trying to determine the cause for the sudden confusion.

The bus grunted forward.

Pressing the stop button the man stood up, the jaguar almost lost under the white ragged threads of his sleeveless denim jacket. Mel watched him move towards the back exit.

1. Suggest an appropriate title for the extract. ____________________

2. Choose the statements that create the impression that something sinister may happen in the story. (You might have to read the extract again.)
   (A) Mel stared at the black panther across the silver bar.
   (B) The bus pulled back into the stream of traffic.
   (C) He could almost see the claws.
   (D) Then he was lost in the damp, clammy crowd.
   (E) Some fool had dashed through the slow moving traffic.

3. After reading the first few lines, what conclusions did you make about Mel's whereabouts?

   ____

4. The words and descriptions in the extract create a tense, suspenseful mood. What information helps you make this conclusion? (Tick your choices.)

   ☐ the dark night ☐ the bus passengers ☐ the silver bar

   ☐ the tattoo ☐ the foolish pedestrian ☐ the panther's eyes

5. It is reasonable to conclude that Mel knew the tattooed man. ☐ True ☐ False

6. Which person is more likely to be in the story at a later stage?

   ☐ the person who ran across the road ☐ the tattooed man

7. Highlight the words that liken the bus to a work animal. ____________________

Noting Detail—'Old faithful' erupts in space

Detail plays an important part in written works. Details help to give the reader a clearer understanding of the story or the topic. Details can give different types of writing their particular 'flavour' and often allow the reader to draw conclusions (see p. 28). When looking at detail in factual material we must determine whether or not it is appropriate to our purpose or studies (see Relevant and Irrelevant Information, p. 50).

Read the following information from '*Old faithful' erupts in space* by Jeff Hecht.

> In the core of the galaxy Messier 101 something stirs every 11 million years. Astronomers, led by Ward Moody at Brighton Young University in Provo, Utah, say that M101 contains a space 'geyser' that periodically ejects large volumes of gas.
>
> M101 is a typical spiral galaxy about 24 million light years from the Earth, which we view nearly face-on. It appears unremarkable in standard images but when the Moody group looked at M101 through a filter that blocked starlight and highlighted the emissions of interstellar clouds of hydrogen, they saw three knots of gas arranged in an 'S' shape, which appeared to have been shot out from the centre of the galaxy.

The detail gives the reader some idea of just how spectacular this space discovery was.

1. What 'details' suggest that the event described was of gigantic proportions?
   Answer: The vast distances and times involved (24 million light years, every 11 million years).

2. Give one detail that shows that most astronomers thought that M101 was commonplace.

   ____

3. Who, or what, is Brighton Young? ______________________________

Continue your reading of *'Old faithful' erupts in space*.

> Active galaxies also eject material from their cores, but these jets are thought to approach the speed of light. By contrast, the knots of gas in M101 seem to be moving sedately at around 100 kilometres per second. Judging from the knots' positions, the geyser's eruptions occur at intervals of about 11 million years, and in alternate directions, shooting out on opposite sides of M101's core.
>
> The astronomers believe that the eruptions occur as black holes pass back and forth through a bar of gas near M101's centre. The faster eruptions in active galaxies are also thought to be caused by black holes. The sluggishness of the knots in M101 suggest that its black hole must be much smaller than black holes in other galaxies.
>
> 'If it's not a black hole, we are in an even **tighter spot** trying to explain it,' says Moody.

4. What detail tells the reader that M101 is a little different from some other galaxies?
   (A) Its distance from Earth.
   (B) The angle at which it is observed.
   (C) The speed at which its geysers eject.
   (D) Its eruptions are caused by black holes.

5. What makes researchers think that the black hole of M101 is smaller than black holes of active galaxies? ______________________________

6. How fast is material being ejected from M101's core? ______________________________

7. The phrase *tighter spot* means ______________________________

8. How confident is Moody of his explanation? ☐ highly ☐ moderately ☐ not very

9. What shape is a typical galaxy? ______________________________

LIFT-OUT
ANSWER SECTION

Answers

Text Types—An Overview

Page 1: Literary Texts: 1. e.g., William Shakespeare 2. Narratives 3. Tells a story with a start, middle and end.

Factual Texts: 1. e.g., Anne Frank 2. Recounts 3. Postcards recount what has happened on someone's holiday. 4. Expositions 5. Its aim is to persuade people.

Understanding Questions

Page 2: Hypnotism 1. Answers may vary. (Hypnotists have less power than originally thought.) 2. TV show volunteers are often willing to be hypnotised. Research by psychologists has cast doubt on the popularly held beliefs. Hypnotists are generally believed to have special powers. 3. False 4. the willingness of the volunteer. 5. Answers will vary.

Page 3: Freeflyers: Modern Skydivers 1. Freeflying—greater control is needed. 2. 300 km/h 3. less than one minute 4. creating formations 5. True 6. daring 7. Answers may vary. (They create difficult manoeuvres in a group.) 8. sensational 9. conventional 10. False (probably a sports magazine)

Page 4: Cloze Exercises

1. (B) but 2. (C) from 3. (D) were

> As he ran for the school bus he felt great, not just because he was getting away from school and going home after a difficult day, (1) **but** because the run itself was exhilarating. It was a break from that prison they called school. The driver smiled as he jumped to the steps just as the door closed and he said, "Made it!"
>
> He was surprised when she replied. "You look as if you just escaped (2) **from** a gang of kidnappers."
>
> People in Sydney don't make light conversation any more, he thought. Haven't got the time. Or too scared they'll get reported for something silly, like being friendly. His smile widened as the bus pulled into the line of traffic.
>
> Things (3) **were** looking better already.

4. (B) huddled 5. (A) avoid 6. (C) displays 7. (B) move

> At the outdoor cafe people sat (4) **huddled** over small tables to chat, or stretched back and read newspapers; the winter sunshine more important than their coffee and cakes.
>
> It was already late morning and Michael was hungry. He kept moving to (5) **avoid** suspicion, walking slowly past shop windows examining the (6) **displays**. Harry's cafe was reflected in the glass. A couple of girls Michael knew had settled themselves on a planter box near the tables, and were slyly observing the customers.
>
> A taxi turned the corner and pulled into the kerb. A smartly dressed woman reached forward to pay the driver then she pushed open the taxi door. As she stepped onto the pavement the girls made their (7) **move**. As carelessly as unhurried shoppers, as carefully as jewel thieves, they moved towards the woman. It was all over before anyone saw what had happened.

8. with stealth.

Page 5: Multiple-Choice Questions—Circles 1. (A) 2. (A) 3. (C) 4. (B) 5. **1.** Elizabeth Costello leaves her childhood home. **2.** The sons dig their mother's grave. **3.** John Costello dies. **4.** The narrator begins his writing.

Finding Facts

Page 6: Polar Ice 1. frazel ice 2. Most icebergs are found in the Antarctic waters 3. nine tenths 4. (D) 5. plough through pack ice 6. False

Page 7: Newspaper Article—Mystery at Mandurah 1. getting ready for the crayfishing season. 2. the Avaneta 3. (D) 4. Answers may vary. 5. (B) 6. It was claimed the police weren't committed to solving the mystery.

Page 8: The Tree of Life 1. Husk, water, flesh, shell, 2. Buy pictures of them 3. It provides necessities for life—food, fuel, shelter, clothing, household products and income. 4. False 5. False 6. True 7. long lasting 8. one of the world's great trees 9. Answers will vary.

Page 9: The Tommy Tycho Story 1. Answers may vary. (autobiography, narrative, personal recount) 2. (C) 3. (A) Growing up with music. 4. True 5. False 6. Answers will vary. (fortunate) 7. distinguished 8. Answers may vary. (successful, fulfilling) 9. Vienna (Austria)/Budapest (Hungary)

Page 10: Fictional Writing—Night of the Muttonbirds 1. Matthew 2. a younger brother 3. the late arrival of the plane 4. agitated 5. (B) 6. False 7. the pilot 8. Mr Trent

Page 11: Our Neighbour in Space 1. Answers may vary. (Springtime on Mars)

2. (a) With the advent of spring — (a) sunlight begins to shine on the ice cap.
(b) By late January — (c) sand dunes are concealed under a frost cover.
(c) Before July — (b) the ice cap has shrunk.

3. True 4. False 5. Mars' ice and snow is formed from carbon dioxide, not water.
6. The winds persistently come from the same direction. 7. (B)

Finding the Main Idea

Page 12: Native Animals as Pets 1. (C) 2. (D) 3. False 4. Native fauna regulations 5. Proper care for native animals/protection for our native animals.

Page 13: Earth First 1. The consumption/use of resources has become a concern. 2. luxuries. 3. Answers may vary: the practice of using a lot of resources. 4. Commercial packaging is becoming common in developing countries as well as in developed countries. 5. declining 6. In recent decades.
7. Answers may vary: An increase in world-wide consumerism has begun to impact on our environment.

Page 14: Fictional Writing—Land of the Rippling Gold 1. They had looked—and had a dreadful shock. 2. **1.** Wendy's parents have a disagreement **2.** Wendy's mother loses a glove. **3.** The windscreen is shattered. **4.** Edie's face is cut. 3. herself (Wendy) 4. a dressing 5. The accident 6. True 7. False 8. False 9. Parent/Teacher to check. Answers may vary. (Wendy—told from her point of view.)

Page 15: Poetry—Bush Medicine. 1. (B) 2. (A) 3. (B) 4. (D) 5. (B) 6. (C) 7. Answers may vary. (respect) 8. Answers may vary. (Traditional ways should be respected.)

Page 16: Stereotypes and Work 1. nine 2. In the world of work, it is easy to be influenced by these fixed concepts and stereotypes. 3. Answers may vary. Parent/Teacher to check. (Stereotyping/TV/fixed ideas) 4. (B) 5. Answers may vary. (Things are changing for the better.) 6. Changing attitudes 7. nobody 8. True 9. Parent/Teacher to check.

Page 17: The Band 1. Answers may vary. (enjoying the music/excitement at a concert/a great experience/etc) 2. (A) 3. A stunning act 4. Once they had finished, they began another of their hits, and then another. 5. False 6. True 7. a bracket (collection) of songs 8. an enthusiastic 9. Any two of the following: applause, clapping, stamping, whistling, shouting, yelling.

What's the Inference?

Page 18: Streetscape 1. Answers may vary. (They were looking for a way to break in. /They didn't want to be seen. etc.) 2. Nicole and Michael remained calm. They operated without undue discussion. They were not nervous. /They knew about alarms/ etc. 3. With descriptions of trying not to be seen or heard. The reader keeps expecting something to happen. 4. the alarm was set. 5. secretly and quietly 6. They knew how to reach the balcony.

Page 19: The Lady in Black 1. foreboding 2. Answers may vary. (detached) 3. Answers may vary. (threatening/secure, alien/familiar, known/unknown) 4. Brett sees movement in the bushes. 5. ghost town gloom, leached life, skeletal. 6. Answers may vary. (To take passengers to their destination. / Complete the journey.) 7. indifference

Page 20: Odious Underarmus, Marathon Man 1. Answers may vary. (school students) 2. (D) 3. (A) 4. They both relate to fishing. (They are puns.) 5. Answers may vary. (Their names all start with 's'. Many are not likely to be fish common to ancient Greece. There is a very wide variety offered. Some of the audience may find some of the fish offered as a little 'unacceptable'.) 6. (B) 7. promised

Page 21: Comics—Politically Correct 1. pet shop owner 2. Parent/Teacher to check. 3. Answers may vary. (He is indifferent to cruelty to animals./He is not very sensitive./He is weary of his job.) 4. pet shop owner 5. (A) 6. Answers may vary. (the ethics of caging birds/cruelty to animals)

Page 22: An Interview with Victor Marshall 1. (A) 2. sympathetic 3. That would be the end of his career. 4. cordial 5. True 6. Answers may vary. (respect/appreciate/feel confident in/value)

Page 23: Book Review—Code of Deception 1. (A) 2. librarians 3. (C) 4. Dr Mulder believes Jake's grandfather stole the plans for an electronic game from him. 5. Answers may vary. (evil, sinister, malevolent, revengeful, etc.) 6. consumed by hate 7. Parent/Teacher to check. 8. **1.** The plans for an electronic game are stolen. **2.** Carson's family company is destroyed. **3.** At fifteen, Jake is a computer genius and swimming coach. 9. By using real encounters with death.

Using Context Clues

Page 24: The Incredible Experience of Megan Kingsley 1. (B) 2. Answers may vary. She didn't want Annabel upset by what might be the truth. 3. Her faced was pressed into Megan's shoulder. 4. Nervousness/tension/fear/worry 5. False 6. about five. She was interested in a cubby./She was concerned about the island blowing away. 7. Parent/Teacher to check. (e.g. to avoid upsetting Annabel unnecessarily)

Page 25: The Second Plane 1. Tapped his ventilator/frowned/forced a smile/couldn't concentrate on his book. 2. Bandierante 3. Answers may vary. (relaxed/happy) 4. Answers may vary (She smiled at Aaron, she was going on holidays (looking at tourist leaflet).) 5. Holiday plans. 6. Was reading without thinking about the meaning. 7. True 8. True 9. Answers may vary. Mystery/suspense/adventure.

Page 26: Special Day 1. (A) 2. (D) 3. (A) 4. (B) 5. (D) 6. (A) 7. (B) 8. Answers will vary. (About 12/13) 9. Parent/Teacher to check. He spent a whole day surfing without parental supervision.

Page 27: Rugby Union 1. impetuous 2. Answers may vary. (It had an unorthodox beginning. People resist change. The rules didn't seem fair.) 3. (B) 4. (2, 1, 4, 3) 5. It had its origins at Rugby School. 6. True

Drawing Conclusions

Page 28: Warbirds over Wanaka 1. (C) 2. Answers may vary. (The number of visitors to Wanaka for the show/the advice to book accommodation well in advance/the number of exhibits at the show.) 3. peaceful 4. Wanaka Warplanes 5. There is a wide variety of machinery/vehicle exhibits. 6. False 7. a positive

Page 29: Recipes—Puddings 1. (A) 2. Answers will vary. (They most likely originated before modern cooking methods were readily available in the country.) 3. (D) 4. (C) 5. (A) 6. Answers may vary. Parent/Teacher to check. (The ingredients have a long shelf life without special storage conditions.) 7. (C) 8. Answers may vary. (cheap, basic) 9. Billy Can Pudding

Page 30: Tsunami 1. (C) 2. True 3. reach shallow water, have their origins close to the shore 4. keeping watch 5. False 6. Japanese 7. volcanic explosion, underground earthquake 8. 1883: Java and Sumatra 9. high

Page 31: Fiction—The Tattooed Man 1. Parent/Teacher to check. 2. (A), (C) 3. That he was at the zoo. 4. the dark night, the tattoo, the panther's eyes 5. False 6. The tattooed man. 7. The bus grunted forward.

Noting Detail

Page 32: 'Old faithful' erupts in space 1. 24 million light years, every 11 million years 2. it appears unremarkable/a typical spiral galaxy 3. a university 4. (C) 5. The speed of the eruptions is much slower. 6. 100 km/sec 7. a more difficult situation 8. moderately 9. spiral

Page 33: Global Warming—Technology for the Environment 1. Ancient: ice caps expand/generally of natural cause/happened slowly/rainforests turned to deserts; Recent: an increase in greenhouse gases. 2. False 3. increasing 4. Industrial Revolution 5. human activity 6. lifestyles 7. floods, droughts 8. use 9. smaller

Page 34: Marauding Elephants Feel the Heat 1. Jack Birochak developed a pepper spray to deter bears. / Loki Osborn is developing a spray to deter elephants. 2. Birochak 3. Cambridge 4. True 5. True 6. False 7. False 8. It deters elephants but is harmless to them. 9. animals 10. grizzly bears 11. keen

Following Directions

Page 35: Pineapple Scones 1. 2 scones 2. Answers will vary. (about 45 minutes) 3. lightly and quickly beaten 4. drained 5. served warm with butter and jam 6. bowl, baking tray, spoon, whisk, knife 7. a brand name for jam

Page 36: Making a Paper Glider 1. instructions (plans, method) 2. **2.** Place the paper clips evenly along one of the short sides of the A4 paper. **3.** Fold the paper in half. **4.** Fold each side in half again to form the wings. 3. (A) 4. snip 5. Materials 6. To show how to make a paper glider. 7. Answers may vary. (Most people prefer to follow diagrams.)

Page 37: Lawn Mower Care Guide 1. (C) 2. (C) 3. (A) 4. yearly 5. mower owners maintain their machines 6. weekly check

Page 38: Recipe—Curried Sausages 1. Answers may vary. (make the instructions easier to follow / make the package more attractive / make the instructions appear simple) 2. Answers may vary. (a trade name / good old-fashioned quality food) 3. (D) 4. **1.** Prick the sausages, **2.** Place the ingredients in a dish, **3.** Prepare the recipe mix, **4.** Add the creamy recipe mixture. 5. one and a half (1.5) 6. False 7. Parent/teacher to check. Answers will vary. 8. Parent/Teacher to check. Answers may vary. 9. traditional, hearty, delicious, creamy, smothered, new 10. covered

Understanding Paragraphs

Page 39: The Incredible Experience of Megan Kingsley 1. (a. 1, b. 2, c. 2, d. 2)
2. on the open sea 3. on the deck of the launch—the bow 4. There has been a change in speakers.
5. Teachers to check. (Megan. We don't know why she was sitting silently). 6. moving/feeling
7. Patrick said that he was hungry and asked for something to eat.

Page 40: Newspaper Article—Mystery at Mandurah 1. Yes 2. Answers will vary. (P1. when it happened, P2. Jim Spice remembers, P3. boat failed to return, P4. search found nothing, P5. boat's unseaworthiness, P6. discovery of equipment) 3. Answers may vary. (to grab reader's attention/make it quick and easy to read/ increase sensationalism) 4. Answers may vary. Jim Spice said, "I remember the day when I went to meet Gill's vessel, the Avaneta, at the Government jetty." 5. discovered/found. 6. Parent/Teacher to check. (Tragedy at Sea, Local Fishermen Disappear, Town's Great Loss) 7. to give it importance/increase impact

Page 41: **Paragraph Breaks** Answers may vary.

Patricia Turner

Patricia Turner was born on 2 December 1939 in Marrickville, Sydney. / Her parents were living in country New South Wales before she was born.//

Soon after Patricia was born, she and her parents moved to an outer suburb of Brisbane. In those days, outer suburbs were more like country towns than urban areas. / It was here she came to love the freedom rural life offered. //

When she was six she attended the local primary school. /There were less than fifty pupils enrolled at the school in those days, most of them the sons and daughters of local farmers. //

Many years later she returned to the school. /As she walked in the gate she could see the changes. / More students, more teachers, more buildings. /And she was the new Principal.

Night of the Muttonbirds

Matthew shifted restlessly in his chair and glanced up at the schoolroom clock on the wall opposite. / Ten-thirty already! / What had happened? / Had something gone wrong? / Today was mail day but the plane was later than usual, and on this of all days when his grandmother, Annie, was returning from hospital in Tasmania. / In nervous anticipation he sat staring out of the window, chewing his fingernails, listening, waiting. //

"Matthew!" Mr Trent's voice was sharp. //

Matthew glanced at him in exasperation, sighed and made a half-hearted attempt to concentrate on the subject in front of him. / Then, to his enormous relief, he heard it, at first indistinct but unmistakable. / The low steady drone of an aircraft approaching. / He stood up pushing his books aside. //

"Matthew! /Sit down!" //

"It's coming," said Matthew. / "The plane, I mean. Mr Greg's coming."

Newspaper Article

Students threatened with expulsion or suspension from school will now have the opportunity to have their side of the argument heard before a special 'education' judge. //

The Department of Education has brought in guidelines which will give student a fair hearing in cases where the student feels he or she has not been treated fairly. //

A parent group from the north coast of NSW said that this change was long overdue. //

However, groups supporting greater discipline in schools disagree, saying that students now have too many rights and genuine learners are being disadvantaged. //

Ms Kathy Kane, spokesperson for the Department said she welcomed the change. //

The new guidelines will come into effect from the beginning of the new school year.

Conversation

"I heard that, Michelle!" said Ms Wright. / "Stand up!"//

"Who me?" / I tried to look innocent. / "I didn't say anything!" //

Ms Wright sighed. / She looked up at the ceiling then back at me. / "It was a ventriloquist, was it?" //

I really don't like those sorts of questions. / Agree, and you are being cheeky—or rude. / Disagree, and you get laughed at by the class.

Recognising Persuasion

Page 42: Rapid Ride 1. yourself 2. Ride the rapids with Rapid Ride 3. True 4. families will be more inclined to go on the ride. 5. Yes 6. race, exhilarating, blood-pumping, unbelievable, tumbling etc.

Page 43: Hogmanay 1 the Viking invaders 2 if you are asked to be the 'first foot' 3. (C) 4. a joyous community event for all 5. 'take a cup o' kindness yet, for auld lang syne' 6. B 7. happily join in any New Year celebrations

Page 44: Earth First 1. pleasant, wealthy 2. (B) 3. bread 4. Buy one, get one free. Hurry before time runs out. 5. Answers may vary. (serviettes, milk bottles, babies, nappies, etc.) 6. Parent/Teacher to check. 7. An ideal way of life.

Page 45: Fake Websites 1. (B) 2. (B) 3. People who create fake websites (for scamming purposes). 4. https and padlock symbols 5. (D) 6. fact 7. a very obvious feature/characteristic 8. To alert the reader to a serious problem/attract the reader's full attention

Fact or Opinion?

Page 46: Shaping the News 1. strongly approving/biased 2. I think 3. opinion 4. opinion 5. fact 6. False 7. Answers may vary. (The poor reporting of important events (wars) on the news.)

Page 47: Shopping Trolleys 1. Poor supervision by parents may be as much to blame for the accident. / Children should ride in a separate carrier. 2. True 3. A separate survey has shown that 80% of parents leave their child unattended./They [paediatricians] think the child should be closer to the ground (Note: it is a fact that the paediatricians hold this opinion)./The child's seat, located high on the trolley, gives the trolley a high centre of gravity. 4. think, suggest 5. False 6. Parent/Teacher to check. Answers will vary. (like, believe/accept the information) 7. False

Page 48: Stereotypes—That's a Job for Me! 1. Luckily things are changing! 2. Fact 3. Fact 4. Fact 5. True 6. Answers may vary. (like/believe) 7. Parent/Teacher to check.

Page 49: Global Warming—Technology for the Environment 1. (C) 2. Fact 3. No. 4. It's too speculative/ Ongoing event rather than 'new', attention-grabbing event/Text is too dense for front page. 5. False 6. (C) 7. Animals do not use technology.

Relevant and Irrelevant Information

Page 50: Snakes and Ladders 1. Sometimes the counters are called 'men'.

Warbirds over Wanaka 2. (B) 3. the size of the crowd. 4. False 5. False

Page 51: iPhoneography 1. Some iPhones are very attractive. 2. the light is behind the photographer 3. (C) 4. False 5. darken the image. 6. the zoom facility is used. 7. special apps

Page 52: Advertisements—Iga Warta Ad 1. the Aboriginal experience 2. True 3. smiling faces 4. the cost 5. The Iga Warta Experience—authentic Aboriginal tourism 6. False (it's for campers) 7. land

Understanding and Using Tables of Contents

Page 53: Touch and Feeling 1. pp. 28–29 2. False. These are other books on the same topic, not necessarily books mentioned in the text. 3. Feelings 4. glossary 5. pp 24–25 6. Index 7. Sensitivity

Page 54: The Age of Dinosaurs in Australia 1. page 34 2. The Dinosaurs of Darkness 3. Suggested reading for more information, Bibliography 4. Index 5. False 6. False 7. True 8. Australia 9. The age of dinosaurs in Australia

Understanding and Using Indexes

Page 55: Technology for the Environment 1. pages 40 to 41 2. two (42 to 46, and 48) 3. recycling 4. six 5. climate 6. Electricity/nuclear energy/fossil fuels. 7. page 19 (from 19 to 20) 8. salty

Page 56: Shaping the News 1. page 6 2. an illustration 3. 25 4. Cave (Peter) 5. alphabetical order 6. False 7. True 8. Answers may vary. (**Radio** has more pages of information than **crime**.) 9. are two

Using Timetables

Page 57: TV Guide 1. WBN 2. 1 hr 25 min 3. No 4. WBN 5. Parent guidance (recommended) 6. 8.30 7. Comet 8. No 9. True 10. False 11. 4 hr 50 min 12. Sports Scene 13. nothing (free) 14. WBS 15. Comet

Page 58: Bega Valley Mobile Library Service Timetable 1. Tuesday 2. (D) 3. (A) 4. Pambula, Tathra, Wyndham 5. 6 hours 6. public holiday 7. True 8. Wyndham

Reading Maps

Page 59: The Oaks Town and Locality Map 1. (C) 2. (D) 3. (D) 4. G6 5. William St and Monkey Creek 6. Cedar Pl 7. Drive, Place, Lane, Road, Street 8. About 2 km

Page 60: Antarctica 1. seven 2. Australia 3. It is divided by a small French claim 4. 1000 km 5. (A) 6. New Zealand 7. (D) 8. Argentina and Britain 9. Casey

Interpreting Tables, Charts and Graphs

Page 61: What authors get when a book is sold 1. False 2. Bookshops. Higher returns per book. 3. bookseller 4. $3.80 5. $2.00 6. True 7. Table 1. 8. Use of the word 'might'. 9. the distributor

Page 62: Seasons and Climate in Antarctica 1. (D) 2. coastal/summer 3. on the Antarctic coast 4. 45 °C 5. 105 °C 6. (B) 7. summer

Page 63: Road Casualties Graphs 1. (D) 2. (A) 3. (B) 4. True 5. 850 6. Answers may vary. (Older people don't walk as often/are more careful when crossing.) 7. (B) 8. Parent/Teacher to check. (Driving a car is the most dangerous form of transport/People become more careful road users as they get older.)

Reading Picture Narratives

Page 64: For Better or For Worse 1. (beard shadow on face/black lines under eyes/mother preparing for bed) 2. realising he has a problem 3. Answer may vary. Reasons may vary. 4. mother – alarm; son – relief), 5. the mother 6. (D) 7. Answers may vary. (Parents don't understand teenagers / adults don't understand what is important / parents don't understand computers.)

Page 65: Hagar the Horrible 1. (C) 2. (C) 3. unconcern, responsibility, anger 4. He is not very aggressive—Viking-like. 5. (B) 6. employment techniques/aggressive behaviour/matching people with the right job

Understanding Plot

Page 66: 1. Answers may vary. (Bears exit home. Goldilocks enters bears' home. Goldilocks damages bears' property, goes to sleep. Bears return. Goldilocks escapes.) 2. Bears find Goldilocks asleep in Baby Bear's bed. 3. Answers will vary. (When Goldilocks breaks something belonging to Baby Bear.)

4. The mouse. The mouse frees the lion before he is killed/taken away 5. The Hare and the Tortoise. 6. Answers may vary. (Never give up. Slow and steady wins the race.)

Testing General Comprehension

Page 67: 'Indian' War Club 1. (A) 2. (B) 3. The Lovoni people were defeated in a war, bought by a circus, brought to America. 4. oddities/savages/less than human) 5. Answers may vary. (sad/upset) 6. (2, 4, 3, 1) 7. (A) 8. souvenirs 9. (C) 10. Answers may vary. (They treated them as slaves.) 11. (C) 12. True 13. False 14. A (Fijian) priest. 15. Europe 16. after 1960 17. A Fijian throwing club 18. Answers may vary. (unfortunate/savages/wild/rescued)

Noting Detail—Global Warming: Technology for the Environment

from *Technology for the Environment* by Mike Callaghan and Peter Knapp

The Earth's climate has changed over millions of years. Places that were once rainforests are now deserts; places which are now on the tops of mountains, hundreds of kilometres from the sea, were once on the ocean floor. Sometimes the climatic changes have been small and could only be noticed by sensitive scientific instruments. At other times they have been extreme.

The ice ages are an example of climatic change. Ice from the polar regions expanded, reaching areas thousands of kilometres away. During the last ice age, humans had to change their lifestyles greatly. They used technology such as fire, the ability to make clothing and shelter, and most importantly, the capacity to think and solve problems to ensure their survival. Animals that could not change or move to warmer regions died.

For millions of years climatic changes were due to natural causes rather than the activities of human beings. However, since the Industrial Revolution over 200 years ago, the actions of people and their use of machines has had a greater and greater effect on the world's climate. Perhaps the greatest influence has been the greenhouse effect.

The amount of greenhouse gases released into the atmosphere since the Industrial Revolution has increased hugely. This is because of the increased use of cars, the clearing and burning of forests, the way people use the planet for food production, and the way people live, using appliances such as air-conditioners and heaters. The greenhouse gases that are the result of human activities rise into the atmosphere and act like a blanket to decrease the amount of radiated heat.

In Australia, scientists predict that there will be a rise in the sea levels with more floods and droughts, and the snowline in the snow field of NSW and Victoria will recede. Parts of inland Australia will receive more rainfall and the cyclone belt of Northern Australia will move further south. There is also the prediction that these changes will affect Australia's energy resources, agriculture and tourist industries. The transport we use, the way we communicate and even our health may be affected.

1. Climatic change has been a feature of the climate since the Earth was formed. Draw lines from *Ancient* or *Recent* to show the features of such climatic change.

   Ancient

   Recent

   - an increase in greenhouse gases
   - generally of natural cause
   - happened slowly
   - rainforests turned to deserts
   - ice caps expand

2. If the Earth gets warmer there will be more deserts. ☐ True ☐ False

   Using one or two words complete these three sentences about the greenhouse effect.

3. The amount of greenhouse gases in the atmosphere is ______________________________.
4. The greenhouse problem began with the ______________________________.
5. Greenhouse gases are a result of ______________________________.

   Find words in the extract to complete these sentences.

6. Humans had to change their ____________ during the last ice age.
7. Scientists predict that there will be more ______________ and ______________.
8. Humans survived the ice ages because they had the ability to _________ technology.
9. Scientists predict the NSW and Victorian snowfield will get (colder smaller deeper).

Noting Detail—Marauding Elephants Feel the Heat

by Jonathan Beard

A pepper spray that deters elephants from raiding farms is being developed by a **zoologist** at the University of Cambridge and an inventor in USA.

"In Asia, elephants destroy thousands of dollars worth of crops each year," says Loki Osborn, the Cambridge zoologist. The problem is also increasing in Africa, says Osborn, as elephants are attracted to this rich source of food.

On both continents, the traditional way of combating the problem is to try to frighten the animals away by shouting at them, beating drums and throwing rocks. Elephants that raid crops are shot. "In Zimbabwe, at least a hundred elephants are killed each year during problem animal control actions," says Osborn, "but this does little to reduce crop damage."

Osborn is working with Jack Birochak, an inventor based at Valley Forge, USA, who has developed pepper sprays to deter grizzly bears. The spray can holds about one kilogram of a mixture of chilli pepper and oil.

Because of the obvious difficulties of operating a spray can close to a wild elephant, Birochak is developing a compressed air launcher that can throw the can as far as two hundred metres. The launcher is aimed at an area near the elephants, and when the can hits the ground it begins spraying. Alternatively, it can be set to start spraying in mid-air.

Tests on wild elephants in Zimbabwe have shown that pepper spray does work. "The elephant, with its long nose lined with mucous membranes, has one of the most **acute**—and sensitive—senses of smell in the animal kingdom," Osborn says. In the tests, he says, the elephants would first freeze, then blow their noses before leaving quickly. The chilli causes no permanent harm.

Osborn hopes that tests of the compressed air launcher in Cambridge will be successful. "The next step will be to test it on elephants in Zimbabwe this summer."

1. Draw a line to match the details that apply to each person.

Loki Osborn is developing	a spray to deter elephants.
Jack Birochak developed	a pepper spray to deter bears.

2. Who is developing the spray can launcher? ____________________

3. The compressed air spray can launcher will be first tested in

☐ Cambridge. ☐ Pennsylvania. ☐ Zimbabwe. ☐ Asia.

4. Elephants have one of the most sensitive animal noses. ☐ True ☐ False

5. Shouting at elephants is used to protect crops. ☐ True ☐ False

6. Elephants are raiding farms to escape pepper-can attacks. ☐ True ☐ False

7. The elephant-deterring sprays are being developed in Africa. ☐ True ☐ False

8. Why do you think the pepper spray is being developed? ____________________

____

9. A *zoologist* is a person who studies ____________________.

10. Pepper spray has been successfully used on ____________________.

11. In the passage, the word *acute* could best be replaced with

☐ *pointed.* ☐ *keen.* ☐ *crucial.* ☐ *brisk.*

Following Directions—Pineapple Scones

If we want to know how to do something we have to follow a **procedure** or, as some people say, **follow directions** or **instructions**. You may have books at home that tell you how to do things. Books with many sets of directions are called **manuals**. Some people have manuals for making repairs. They can be called **how-to** books.

Some directions/instructions are simple. A machine at a ferry terminal has **instructions** on how to purchase a ticket. We call each part of the directions (instructions) a **step**. People follow directions nearly every day of their lives.

Directions/instructions have two basic forms:

1. Some instructions follow a sequence of steps to achieve a goal. Examples include recipes, 'how to' put things together, 'how to' play games, and so on. Diagrams are often used to supplement the written instructions.
2. Other instructions are not set out in sequential form. Examples include instructions on 'how to' care for a car or 'how to' enjoy a holiday.

Read this **recipe** for pineapple scones. (NB: The word **recipe** is not restricted to cooking instructions.)

Pineapple Scones ← The aim/goal (what you will make)

Serves 4 ← How many people you will be catering for

Ingredients (Often called *materials needed* in instructions other than recipes)

2 cups of self raising flour
½ cup water
450 g can crushed pineapple, drained
1 tablespoon of caster sugar
1 egg
1 tablespoon caster sugar, extra
30 g butter or margarine
1 tablespoon powdered milk
½ tablespoon mixed spices

Method ← The steps (or instructions) you must follow. They are in the order you do them.

1. Sift flour into a large bowl. Stir in sugar. Rub in butter.
2. **Whisk** together water, egg and powdered milk. Mix into flour mixture with a knife. Lightly mix in crushed pineapple.
3. Shape dough mixture into a round. Place on a well greased baking tray. Make impressions in the dough with a knife to form 8 wedges.
4. Bake at 220°C for 25 to 30 minutes or until scone sounds hollow when tapped.
5. Sprinkle top with combined sugar and spices while hot. ← Concluding step

Serve warm with butter and Mrs Farmer's jam of choice. ← Concluding statement

1. This recipe makes _____ pineapple scones for each person to be served. ____________________
2. About how long do you estimate it would take to prepare pineapple scones? ____________________
3. Describe what is done when something is *whisked*. ____________________

____

4. Before the pineapple crush can be used, it must be ____________________.
5. It is recommended that pineapple scones be ____________________.
6. Name three cooking utensils required to make pineapple scones.

______________ ______________ ______________

7. Who or what do you think Mrs Farmer is? ____________________

Following Directions—Making a Paper Glider

Look at these instructions for constructing a paper glider. You will find that it will fly better than **traditional** paper gliders.

What you will need

I sheet of A4 paper
4 paper clips
a pair of scissors

Directions

1. Take a sheet of A4 paper
2. . . . .?
3. . . . .?
4. . . . .?
5. Make two **small cuts** on the fold lines in the tail.
6. Fold the flaps up.

Now it is time to test fly your glider.

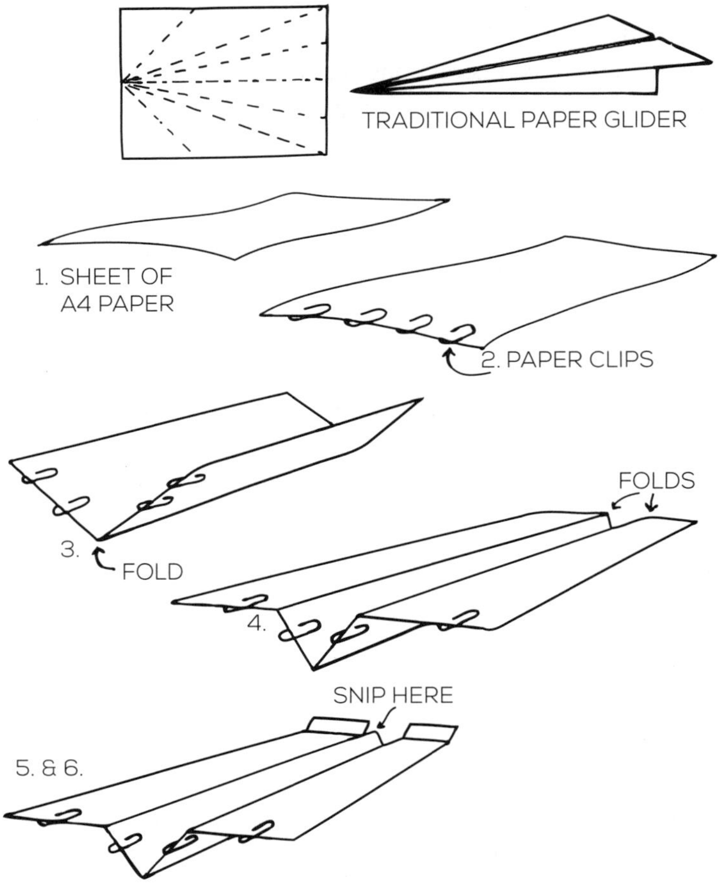

TRADITIONAL PAPER GLIDER

1. SHEET OF A4 PAPER

2. PAPER CLIPS

3. FOLD

FOLDS

4.

SNIP HERE

5. & 6.

1. The word *directions* could best be replaced with the word ________________ .

2. The directions are incomplete. Looking at the diagram above, complete instructions 2, 3 and 4 on these lines.

2. ____ .

3. ____ .

4. ____ .

3. In the introduction, the word *traditional* could best be replaced with the word
(A) *usual.* (B) *popular.* (C) *historical.* (D) *common.*

4. What is the word for a *small cut* with a pair of scissors? a ________________

5. The best word to replace the heading *What you will need* would be
☐ ingredients. ☐ materials. ☐ components. (Tick one box.)

6. What is the aim of these instructions? ________________

7. The written instructions are easier to follow than the diagrams. ☐ True ☐ False

Following Directions—Lawn Mower Care Guide

These instructions differ from the earlier examples. The sequence in which owners follow the instructions/directions is not critical. The reader has some options as to how or when each instruction will be followed.

Your Keys to Trouble-Free Year-Long Lawn Mowing

Keep this guide with your mower tool kit for quick reference.

Weekly Checks
- Engine oil level.
- Fuel in tank. (Do not check while engine is running.)
- Spark plug—remove and clean.
- Clean mower deck and external fittings. (Do not use hose.)

Monthly Checks
As for weekly checks plus:
- Mower blades. (Always have a spare set of blades.)
- Oil filter.
- Air filter—clean if dirty.
- Tighten all bolts and screws.
- Grass-catcher. (Hose out accumulated build-up, clean air vents.)
- Fuel line for leaks.
- Remove build-up of grass/dirt under chassis.
- Height adjustment fittings.

Six-Monthly Checks
(or as specified by manufacturer)
- Replace oil filter and oil.
- Change air cleaner element.
- Replace spark plug.
- Chassis for cracks.
- Throttle cable for wear.
- Replace worn blades.
- Tighten blade plate.
- **Lubricate** exposed parts, moving parts and handle joints.
- Check exhaust for corrosion.

1. Which one of the following does NOT need to be checked at a **monthly check**?
(A) spark plug
(B) engine oil level
(C) exhaust
(D) mower blades

2. The word **lubricate** in Six-Monthly Checks means to
(A) replace damaged or worn parts.
(B) loosen all parts that have movable adjustments.
(C) apply oil to improve ease of operation and control.
(D) check for safety of any parts affected by vibrations.

3. Which of these 'checks' is in order from most often to least often?
(A) fuel in tank, clean oil filter, replace worn blades
(B) exhaust corrosion, clean grass-catcher, remove and clean spark plug
(C) replace oil filter, clean mower deck, throttle cable for wear
(D) fuel line, tighten blade plate, remove build-up of grass under chassis

4. How often should the mower blades be changed? ______________________________

5. The aim of these instructions is to help ______________________________.

6. Which checklist least needs the help of a mechanic or service centre? ____________________

Following Directions—Recipe: Curried Sausages

This is a recipe from the back of a curry mix packet.

Use the contents of this *Traditional* pack to make a delicious meal of sausages **smothered** in a mild, creamy curry sauce.

Recipe ingredients

8 thick sausages
1 onion, sliced
2 carrots, diced
1 pkt *Traditional* Curried Sausages recipe mix
1.5 cups water (hot for microwave)
2 tablespoons tomato sauce

Preparation time: 10 minutes
Cooking time: 50–60 minutes

Directions

1. Prick sausages several times with a fork. Place sausages, onion and carrots in dish.

2. Combine *Traditional* recipe mix with water and tomato sauce. Pour into dish and cover.
3. Cook in gas or electric oven at 180°C.

MICROWAVE DIRECTIONS

Prepare as directed and cook on HIGH for 20–25 minutes. For a **hearty** complete meal, serve with peas and creamy mashed potato.

Made in Australia
Best used before 12/10/2014

Makes four 400 g serves

1. What do you think the illustrations are for? ______________________.
2. In this recipe the word *Traditional* refers to ______________________.
3. The word *hearty* in the recipe could be best replaced by
   (A) *cheerful.* (B) *sincere.* (C) *happy.* (D) *satisfying.*
4. Number the boxes (1–4) to show the order in which things should be done.
   ☐ Place the ingredients in a dish. ☐ Prick the sausages.
   ☐ Add the creamy recipe mixture. ☐ Prepare the recipe mix.
5. How many packets of curry mix should be used to make 400 g serves for 6 people? ____________
6. It not important to follow the procedure set out in the recipe. ☐ True ☐ False
7. In your opinion, who is most likely to buy this sort of product? ____________
8. Briefly give reasons for your opinion in question 7. ____________
9. What words in these instructions try to create the impression that this Curry Mix is a good product?
   ____
10. What word (that doesn't have emotional qualities) could *smothered* be replaced with? ____________

Understanding Paragraphs— The Incredible Experience of Megan Kingsley

We had an early look at paragraphs in Finding the Main Idea. Read page 12 again.

New paragraphs indicate the introduction of new circumstances or people into the writing.

New paragraphs usually indicate the introduction of a change of:

- ideas or character
- place/setting/location
- speakers in conversation
- time
- action (what's happening).

Each new paragraph starts on a new line. In some writing it is **indented** (it starts a little bit in from the margin). The space between the paragraphs may be greater than the space between the sentences.

Paragraphs usually contain:
- a topic sentence (see Finding the Main Idea)
- other sentences providing supporting detail
- several sentences.

Single-sentence paragraphs or single-word paragraphs are used for effect (impact) or in speech/conversations. Newspapers have a convention of using single sentence paragraphs.

Read this extract from *The Incredible Experience of Megan Kingsley* by Pamela O'Connor and answer the questions.

The small launch bobbed wildly in the wild choppy water, like a toy duck in a baby's bath, as the captain steered skilfully towards the rocky, forbidding cove of Stellar Island.

To the two small figures sitting in the bow, the cove appeared to have been carved out of the two sheer black cliff faces that rose straight up from the sea. The children laughed suddenly as the cold spray splashed all over them.

"Patrick and Annabel!" their mother called. "Come back here!"

The pair reluctantly left the front of the boat and clambered down the small hatch to the cabin below. Their older sister sat quietly on a bench staring stonily at the water lapping against the porthole.

"What's the matter with Megan?" asked Annabel.

"Nothing," replied their mother. "Just leave her alone."

"I'm hungry," announced Patrick. "Can we have something to eat?"

"We'll be landing in a few minutes. We'll have lunch when we get to the house." Mrs Kingsley frowned as she looked at her elder daughter, wondering how much longer Megan could keep up this stony silence. It was so unlike her.

1. Write the number of sentences in each of these paragraphs.
   (a) Paragraph 1 ______ (b) Paragraph 2 ______ (c) Paragraph 3 ______ (d) Paragraph 4 ______

2. Where is the action in paragraph 1 located? ________________________________

3. Where does the action in paragraph 2 move to? ________________________________

4. Paragraph 6 is a new paragraph because (Tick one box.)
   - ☐ it describes a dramatic change in events.
   - ☐ it introduces a break in time.
   - ☐ the story is getting more interesting.
   - ☐ there has been a change in speakers.
   - ☐ the story has moved to a new location.

5. In your opinion, which character leaves the most unanswered questions in the reader's mind?
   __________ Can you explain why? ________________________________

6. Megan is staring stonily at the water. This means she is staring without ____________________.

7. Rewrite paragraph 7 in indirect speech (as it would be reported in a newspaper). ______________
   ____

Understanding Paragraphs—Newspaper Article: Mystery at Mandurah

Reports usually use indirect speech (reported speech). Read part of the newspaper article 'Mystery at Mandurah' by Jill Burgess again.

In March 1969, a tragedy struck when local fishermen Hugh Gill and Bevan Hahn went fishing for crays and were never seen again.

Resident Jim Spice could recall the day he went to meet Gill's vessel, the Avaneta, at the Government jetty.

But it was an appointment she did not keep.

Gill, 62, and Hahn, 33, were last seen shifting cray pots more than 36 km off Halls Head, but an intensive search by fishermen and a coastal sweep by a flotilla of yachts returning from Bunbury failed to turn up any clues.

The weather was rough and the 22-year-old boat, previously wrecked on the entrance bar, should not have been rebuilt and certainly not have put to sea in the condition it was in.

Later, fisherman Ray Brennan discovered a number of craypots, floats and ropes adrift in the general area of the Avaneta's last sighting.

The floats were clearly marked with the vessel's number and an echo sounder revealed an object the size of the missing vessel 40 m down on the ocean bed.

Convinced it was the Avaneta, Brennan and others marked the spot and spent precious time needed to prepare for the crayfish season guiding police and divers to the spot.

But the search was called off when police claimed their divers were not equipped to do deep dives.

Later in the year, a row was brewing as fishermen and residents claimed police were reluctant to follow a lead which could solve the disappearance.

There were conflicting opinions as to why specialist help was not obtained and the site investigated further.

According to reports, the marker flag was moved when the dive was abandoned and the spot could not later be identified.

A second theory blamed the recent Meekering earthquake, which caused tremors which set the flag adrift and shifted the vessel on the ocean bed.

The marker was eventually found miles away.

But the only clue ever to **come to light** was Gill's fishing box, found on the beach.

1. All of the paragraphs in this article are single-sentence paragraphs. Yes / No
2. In two or three words describe what each of the following paragraphs is about. There may be more than one way of describing what each paragraph is about. The first one has been done for you.

   Paragraph 1: When it happened ________ Paragraph 4: ________

   Paragraph 2: ________ Paragraph 5: ________

   Paragraph 3: ________ Paragraph 6: ________

3. Why do you think newspaper articles use one-sentence paragraphs?

   ____

4. Rewrite the second paragraph in direct speech. (Use quotation marks.) ________

   ____

5. The phrase *come to light* could be replaced by the words 'be ________'.
6. Suggest a newspaper headline suitable for the first reports of this incident in 1969. ________

   ____

7. The third paragraph is short. The effect is ________.

Understanding Paragraphs—Paragraph Breaks

On this page are four exercises in which you are asked to select where the paragraph breaks should be. The extracts have been copied without the breaks in place. A slash has been inserted at the end of each sentence. Use a coloured pencil or highlighter to colour the slash where one paragraph ends and a new paragraph begins.

1. There should be four paragraphs in this extract. Highlight where new paragraphs should begin. (The first one has been done (with a double slash—//) to help you.)

Patricia Turner was born on 2 December 1939 in Marrickville, Sydney. / Her parents were living in country New South Wales before she was born. **//** Soon after Patricia was born, she and her parents moved to an outer suburb of Brisbane. / In those days, outer suburbs were more like country towns than urban areas. / It was here she came to love the freedom rural life offered. / When she was six she attended the local primary school. / There were less than fifty pupils enrolled at the school in those days, most of them the sons and daughters of local farmers. / Many years later she returned to the school. / As she walked in the gate she could see the changes. / More students, more teachers, more buildings. / And she was the new Principal.

2. In this extract from *Night of the Mutton Birds* by Mary Small highlight four places where new paragraphs should start. (There are five paragraphs altogether.)

Matthew shifted restlessly in his chair and glanced up at the schoolroom clock on the wall opposite. / Ten-thirty already! / What had happened? / Had something gone wrong? / Today was mail day but the plane was later than usual, and on this of all days when his grandmother, Annie, was returning from hospital in Tasmania./ In nervous anticipation he sat staring out of the window, chewing his fingernails, listening, waiting. / "Matthew!" Mr Trent's voice was sharp. / Matthew glanced at him in exasperation, sighed and made a half-hearted attempt to concentrate on the subject in front of him. / Then, to his enormous relief, he heard it, at first indistinct but unmistakable. / The low steady drone of an aircraft approaching. / He stood up pushing his books aside. / "Matthew! / Sit down!" / "It's coming," said Matthew. / "The plane, I mean. / Mr Greg's coming."

3. In this extract from a newspaper highlight all places where new paragraphs should start.

Students threatened with expulsion or suspension from school will now have the opportunity to have their side of the argument heard before a special 'education' judge. / The Department of Education has brought in guidelines which will give student a fair hearing in cases where the student feels he or she has not been treated fairly. / A parent group from the north coast of NSW said that this change was long overdue. / However, groups supporting greater discipline in schools disagree, saying that students now have too many rights and genuine learners are being disadvantaged. / Ms Kathy Kane, spokesperson for the Department, said she welcomed the change. / The new guidelines will come into effect from the beginning of the new school year.

4. In this short conversation highlight three places where new paragraphs should start.

"I heard that, Michelle!" said Ms Wright. / "Stand up!" / "Who me?" / I tried to look innocent. / "I didn't say anything!" / Ms Wright sighed. / She looked up at the ceiling then back at me. / "It was a ventriloquist, was it?" / I really don't like those sorts of questions. / Agree, and you are being cheeky—or rude. / Disagree, and you get laughed at by the class.

Recognising Persuasion—Rapid Ride

Almost without being aware of it, we are bombarded with persuasive messages every day. You cannot watch television, listen to the radio or read a magazine without being confronted with advertisements. Advertisements are trying to get you to choose a particular **product** or **service**.

But there are other ways people use persuasion. Your school friends may try to persuade you to join them in an after-school activity. Another student may try to persuade you that he or she is the best person for school captain. These people are trying to persuade you to **think** or **act** in a particular way.

Persuasive writing has some special features:

- it tries to **attract (and hold)** the reader's **attention**
- it may use a mixture of **logical** and **emotive language**
- it sounds **convincing** (as if the writer is an expert) and often has an element of urgency
- it often appears to address the reader/listener **in a personal way**.

Read this advertisement from a tourist magazine and answer the questions.

The world's most exciting Jet Boat ride

Rapid Ride jets bring blood-pumping excitement to your holiday. The year-round sunshine makes Coral Harbour a great place to experience the exhilarating, yet safe, Rapid Ride Jet Fly-Over. The unbelievable speed and manoeuvrability of the jet boats will thrill you as you blast along narrow gorges, over tumbling white rapids and through mangrove tunnels as **you** race for the coast.

Join over 2 million people who have had this experience of a lifetime. Make it a part of **your** Coral Harbour holiday.

During April, ***KIDS ARE FREE*** on ***Rapid Ride*** jets. One child per full-fare paying adult on ***Rapid Ride*** jets rides for ***FREE***.

Conditions apply:

- Child must be aged between 5 and 15.
- Offer only valid Mon to Thurs (school term only).
- Offer not valid in school holidays.

Ride the rapids with Rapid Ride

For further information ring Laura on 012 200 002 between 9 am and 5 pm.

Learning Points

- Speaks to the reader directly by using the words *your* and *you*.
- Attracts the reader's attention with a picture and large type for the heading.
- This ad appeals to the **emotions** more than to common sense (**logic**).
- The ad gives the impression that this could be happening for you right now, just by (your parents) making the right decision.
- The ad is loaded with **colourful words**: 'blood-pumping', 'exhilarating', 'thrill', 'blast'.
- 'You' see yourself (male or female) being part of the ride.
- Being part of two million is an extra incentive—it makes you feel you've been part of a popular event.
- Makes use of a **slogan**.
- Concluding statement (information available).

1. Who are you supposed to think of instead of the people in the jet boat? ____________________

2. What is the slogan used by Rapid Ride? ____________________

3. This ad emphasises a need to act without too much delay. ☐ True ☐ False

4. What do you think will be the effect of the free offer? ____________________

5. As two million people have enjoyed this ride is it assumed that you will also? Yes / No

6. Give two colourful words used in the ad. ____________________ ____________________

Recognising Persuasion—Hogmanay

The Scots have a long, rich heritage associated with New Year's Eve. They call it Hogmanay. Read the text and answer the questions, remembering what you have learned about persuasion.

It is believed that the Scots learned the tradition of Hogmanay from the Vikings, who raided and settled parts of Scotland in the 8th–10th centuries. People living in northern countries have plenty of reason to celebrate the passing of the middle of winter.

Before Hogmanay (31 December) houses are cleaned and ashes are removed from fireplaces. There is also a tradition that all debts should be cleared before 'the bells' ring at midnight.

In some Scottish towns a burning barrel is rolled through the street; in other places an old boat or a straw figure is burned. These customs symbolise the burning of the old year to make way for the new year. It is a day—and a night—of celebration and a joyous community event for all.

On the stroke of midnight everyone joins hands and sings the old song by Robert Burns (1788), 'Auld Lang Syne' (meaning 'old times') and then there is a round of kissing friends and strangers alike and wishing them all a 'guid' New Year. Everyone is encouraged and expected to join in. The underlying purpose of this is to clear out the **vestiges** of the old year, make a clean break and welcome in the young new year on a happy note. This tradition is so popular it has spread around the world.

'First footing' (the first foot in the door after midnight) is still a common practice in Scotland. Traditionally, the 'first foot' should be a young dark-haired male (a blond face at the door probably brought back bad old memories of Viking invaders) bringing gifts—coal, shortbread, salt, black bun or whisky—as symbols of prosperity for the household. These days, if you are asked to be the 'first foot', other symbols of warmth, food and drink are just as acceptable.

An integral part of the Hogmanay partying is to welcome friends and strangers with warm hospitality. If you are invited to celebrate Hogmanay, embrace its spirit and 'take a cup o' kindness yet, for auld lang syne'.

1. The Scottish tradition of Hogmanay began with ________________________.
2. Highlight a phrase where the writer speaks directly to the reader.
3. For the Scots, the burning of goods and items was a
   (A) way to get rid of anything unwanted.
   (B) way of showing friendliness towards strangers.
   (C) symbolic way of starting the year afresh, clearing away the problems of the past year.
   (D) recognition of the passing of the middle of winter.
4. The text uses a mixture of factual statements and opinions. Tick a box to identify an opinion.
   - ☐ a burning barrel is rolled through the street
   - ☐ a joyous community event for all
   - ☐ This tradition is so popular it has spread around the world.
   - ☐ Before Hogmanay (31 December) houses are cleaned.
5. Underline a Scottish toast that is included in the text.
6. The word *vestiges* has a similar meaning to
   (A) valuables (B) remnants (C) variables (D) hardships
7. How does the writer of the text expect a reader to respond to the information? ________________

Recognising Persuasion—Earth First

David Bowden and Jenny Dibley looked at how people are influenced by persuasive advertising.

Why do we consume so much?

Many of us are starting to ask the question: 'Why do I buy so many things?' Can you think back to toys that you have owned? What has happened to them? What about all your friend's toys? Some of them have ended up in the local rubbish tip and many of your toys have not been biodegradable. Think about how much more waste you and your friends will contribute over the next ten years.

Companies have employed many people and spent millions of dollars on advertising; creating new ways to sell products. Some methods used to entice consumers are listed below.

Time-saving devices

Disposable items have become popular in the past twenty years. They are products we use only once, or a few times, then throw away. These disposable products include drink and food containers, razors, tissues, pens and cameras. Disposable products are convenient for busy families. They have been designed to save time for our 'fast-moving society'.

Many disposable products are used at fast-food outlets. When we order a meal it sometimes comes in a polystyrene container, with paper serviettes, plastic eating utensils and a tray with a paper placemat. Our drinks are served in plastic cups and we drink them through a plastic straw. There is often more packaging than food.

Extra, extra

It is common practice to produce items that require accessories that make them 'seem' complete. For example, a doll may have accessories such as clothing which are sold separately. Accessories cost more money and advertisements for them are designed to make us feel that our original purchase is incomplete.

Sale time

Bargain sales are a great way to tempt consumers. Most shops have sales regularly, to move old or discontinued stock. Are there really bargains in these shops or is it just a way to get you to buy the products even if you don't need them?

Most forms of advertising follow a simple format. Advertisements promote a way of life that is presented as ideal. People in advertisements are usually attractive, happy, own expensive cars and houses and generally promote a high standard of living. Is this really how most people live?

'Hurry before they all run out!'

There are many ways of persuading us to consume. Sometimes we shop to the sound of a voice telling us we can get "two for the price of one!" or "hurry before they all run out". We are often told that "an offer like this will never be repeated".
The implication is that we cannot live without these products.

1. People in ads are usually (aged pleasant male wealthy uncooperative). (Circle one answer.)

2. The writers have included questions in the extract. These questions are meant to
   (A) raise issues that need answers.
   (B) develop consumer/reader awareness.
   (C) be answered by the reader.
   (D) help readers with their research.

3. Of the following goods, which is the most likely to use the least advertising for extras?
   ☐ bread ☐ four wheel drive ☐ computer ☐ swimming pool

4. Which advertising techniques from the article above are used in the ad on p. 42? ____________

5. Name one item that has become disposable in recent years. ____________

6. Name a toy that you once owned that didn't come up to its TV image. ____________

7. What do most ads promote? ____________

Recognising Persuasion—Fake Websites

Not all persuasive writing uses techniques that appeal to the reader's emotions, ego or prestige. Some writing tries to persuade us to act or think in a particular way by appealing to our reasoning.

Will you be a victim?

There are many websites that are designed specifically to gain access to people's private and confidential information. These websites can be created by anyone with enough knowledge of website design. Internet scams are very common in the 21st century.

One of the first rules of online security is to exercise caution at all times. Try to avoid clicking on links in pop-up ads or links in emails that seem to be phony or suspicious. A good general rule is to type the website address in your address bar directly, rather than use a link in an email message, especially if you are going to a financial site.

How to identify fake websites and scams

To the inexperienced person, all websites look legitimate. It is hard to tell whether it is safe to input private information; e.g. when purchasing online products. If you are not sure or have doubts about whether the website can be trusted, then **STOP!!!** Take your time to investigate the website further. People who design such websites to gain access to data and scam people are known as '**phishers**'.

When logging onto websites always look out for an 'http', which will be on the URL bar at the top of the screen.

In addition, when logging into a server or buying online items, look for the 'padlock' icon, which will be on the bottom right of the website page.

A **dead giveaway** for a fake URL or a fake website is basic spelling mistakes in the web address itself. Some URLs look very much like the name of a well-known company, but there may be letters transposed or left out. An example might be 'mircosoft.com' instead of 'microsoft.com'. These slight differences can be easy to miss, and that's what phishers are counting on.

1. The writer of the article believes that
(A) fake websites are readily recognised.
(B) most people will come across a fake website.
(C) fake websites are created by unskilled amateurs.
(D) online shopping is not susceptible to fake websites.

2. It is most likely the writer is appealing to the reader's
(A) honesty. (B) reason. (C) frustrations. (D) optimism.

3. What is meant by the term 'phishers'? ______________________________

____

4. Any person can check the genuineness of a website by looking for

____________________ and ____________________.

5. This text could most likely appear in
(A) a computer manual. (B) shopping advertising pamphlets.
(C) a research journal. (D) an internet shopping advice guide.

6. This text is mostly based on (fact opinion). (Tick one option.)

7. What is meant by *dead giveaway*? ______________________________

8. What is the effect of the text in bold (**STOP!!!**)? ______________________________

Fact or Opinion?—Shaping the News

Facts and opinions are part of our everyday speech and writing. It is important to know when someone is using an argument based on their opinion to persuade you to believe or do something. (See Recognising Persuasion, p. 42, and Finding the Facts, p. 6).

A **fact** is something that everyone agrees with. It can usually be proved either by observation or written records. The wording of facts is usually precise. We are often given the source of facts.

An **opinion** is a particular viewpoint of the writer or speaker.

An opinion can:
- be personal
- be used to influence (or convince) the reader or listener with emotive language
- provide suggestions on courses of action (what to do).

Read this extract.

> There are now less than 300 elephants left in lower sections of the valley. These beautiful animals once roamed free across the valley right up to the low foothills of the western range. The uncontrolled slaughter of the elephant herds is to be deplored.

Fact: There are now less than 300 elephants left in lower sections of the valley. This could be proved by doing a count, doing some research and comparing elephant populations over a period of time.
Opinion: These beautiful animals—some people may think they are beautiful but it cannot be proved. It is quite possible many people may have a different opinion.

In **opinionative writing**, the writer expresses a judgement, may make recommendations and has a stated point of view.

> I think all children should play sport. It keeps them healthy and it makes them better people. We all respect our famous sportspeople.
>
> If children don't play sport they grow up lazy and uninterested in life. As they get older they become unfit and have to have medical treatment which is unfair on other members of their families.
>
> The council should spend more money on building pools and sports grounds.

In the above passage it is quite easy to determine the opinions held by the writer.

1. How would you describe the writer's opinion on sport? ______________________

2. What are the first words that 'warn' the reader that this writing is opinion? ______________

Read this extract adapted from *Shaping the News* by John D Fitzgerald.

> Most people enjoy reading about crime, especially violent crime. Stories about bombings, murders, armed robberies that involve large sums of money and serious assaults attract readers, especially if they are local events.
>
> An unusual crime is highly newsworthy. Once it was rare for bank robberies to occur and when they did they were reported in detail. Now there are many more robberies and they tend to be reported in much less detail.
>
> The ultimate act of violent conflict is war between nations. This should be newsworthy. However, unless Australia or its friends are involved, the news reports of the war are only brief.

3. Most people enjoy reading about crime, especially violent crime. (fact opinion)

4. An unusual crime is highly newsworthy. (fact opinion)

5. Once it was rare for bank robberies to occur. (fact opinion)

6. Most of the information in the extract is fact. ☐ True ☐ False

7. What does the writer want the reader to react to? ______________________

Fact or Opinion?—Shopping Trolleys

from 'Why shopping trips end in tears for kids' by Vincent Kiernan

Read the magazine article on this page and answer the questions on **fact and opinion.**

Shopping Trolleys

Supermarket trolleys are responsible for injuring more than 26 000 American children each year, and should be redesigned to make them more stable, say four paediatricians from Ohio State University College of Medicine.

'Shopping carts are not designed for the safe transport of children,' the doctors say in the current issue of the *Archives of Paediatric Medicine.*

Today's trolleys have a narrow wheel base and are prone to tip over. The child's seat, located high on the trolley, gives the trolley a high centre of gravity, making it even more likely to tip, say the researchers. Strapping them in is no protection if the trolley is upset.

So the paediatricians would like to see the shopping trolleys **redesigned** with the wheels positioned further apart. And they **think** the child should ride in a separate carrier attached to the trolley, and closer to the ground.

According to government statistics, some 26 700 children were taken to hospitals for emergency treatment after trolley accidents in 1992. About 43% of them suffered contusions or abrasions. Another 25% had cuts. But 6% had concussion and 2% had broken bones.

Serious injuries do happen. During the three-year period, the team estimates that about 2000 children had to be kept in hospital because of fractures, concussion and internal injuries.

Poor supervision by parents may be as much to **blame** for the accidents as poor trolley design: a separate survey has shown that 80% of parents leave their child unattended at least once while they search the supermarket shelves.

The paediatricians, however, **suggest** that it is probably easier to redesign the trolley than to change the shopping habits of millions of parents.

1. Referring to the above article, tick the boxes that express opinions.

- ☐ Supermarket trolleys are responsible for injuring more than 26 000 American children.
- ☐ Poor supervision by parents may be as much to blame for the accidents.
- ☐ Children should ride in a separate carrier.
- ☐ Today's trolleys have a narrow wheel base.

2. This report contains research facts, but much of the text is opinion. ☐ True ☐ False

3. Tick the boxes which are facts taken from the above extract.

- ☐ A separate survey has shown that 80% of parents leave their child unattended.
- ☐ It is probably easier to redesign the trolley than to change shopping habits.
- ☐ They [paediatricians] think the child should be closer to the ground.
- ☐ The child's seat, located high on the trolley, gives the trolley a high centre of gravity.

4. Which words warn the reader that the information is probably an opinion?

☐ *think* ☐ *redesigned* ☐ *suggest* ☐ *blame*

5. It is a fact that parents' shopping habits cannot be changed. ☐ True ☐ False

6. Because the writer refers to professional sources the reader is likely to ______________ the article.

7. The writer expresses a firm view on trolley safety. ☐ True ☐ False

Fact or Opinion?—Stereotypes: That's a Job for Me!

from *That's a Job for Me!* by Ross Pearce

"Snakes are poisonous! Quick! Kill the snake!"

Many an unfortunate non-venomous snake has been killed because we do not question the truth of our preconceived notions or stereotypes. Stereotypes are fixed ideas or feelings we have about things in our world. They influence much of our thinking. Our actions are often based on the stereotypes we hold in our minds.

In the world of work, it is easy to be influenced by these fixed concepts and stereotypes. "I can't do that job; only boys do that sort of work." "I'd like to do that when I leave school but I think that's a job for women." Such ideas can greatly reduce the jobs we might think suitable for ourselves. They are like invisible chains restricting our freedom to choose from the widest range of jobs. Why do people allow themselves to be robbed of this freedom?

Stereotypes sneak into our minds without us even realising it and then they become part of our way of thinking.

"Jenny loves bandaging cuts and bruises. She's going to be a nurse when she grows up."

"Jason loves bandaging cuts and bruises. He's going to be a doctor when he grows up."

When Jenny and Jason watch television they see that the nurses are usually women and the doctors are usually men. So little Jenny and Jason store in their minds the stereotype that girls become nurses and boys become doctors. They do not remember where the idea came from. They believe that it was what they chose freely for themselves and what they always wanted.

To understand how stereotypes sneak into our thoughts we need to be alert for clues in what people say to us and what we hear, watch and read in the media. Television can be very influential in developing these stereotypes in people's minds.

Luckily things are changing!

People are questioning stereotypes. They are throwing aside old-fashioned ideas that told them there were jobs they could not do. They are breaking free from the chains of stereotypes and doing the jobs they really want to do.

1. Tick the box that is an opinion taken from the above extract.

☐ Stereotypes are fixed ideas or feelings we have about things in our world.

☐ When Jason watches television he sees that the nurses are usually women.

☐ Our actions are often based on the stereotypes we hold in our minds.

☐ Luckily things are changing!

Tick the correct box for the next three questions to indicate if they are fact or opinion.

2. Many a non-venomous snake has been killed. ☐ Fact ☐ Opinion

3. Television can be very influential in developing these stereotypes in people's minds.

☐ Fact ☐ Opinion

4. People are questioning stereotypes. ☐ Fact ☐ Opinion

5. In the writer's opinion, there is still much stereotyping in our society. ☐ True ☐ False

6. Select a word from the text that warns the reader the passage they are reading may be an opinion.

7. Have you have ever held ideas that are based upon stereotypes? **Yes / No**

If you have, can you give one example of this stereotyping? (No written answer is required.)

Fact or Opinion?—Global Warming: Technology for the Environment

from *Technology for the Environment* by Mike Callaghan and Peter Knapp

The Earth's climate has changed over millions of years. Places that were once rainforests are now deserts; places which are now on the tops of mountains, hundreds of kilometres from the sea, were once on the ocean floor. Sometimes the climatic changes have been small and could only be noticed by sensitive scientific instruments. At other times they have been extreme. The ice ages are an example of climatic change. Ice from the polar regions expanded, reaching areas thousands of kilometres away. During the last ice age, humans had to greatly change their lifestyles. They used technology such as fire, the ability to make clothing and shelter, and most importantly, the capacity to think and solve problems to ensure their survival. Animals that could not use technology or move to warmer regions died as the climate changed.

For millions of years climatic changes were due to natural causes rather than the activities of human beings. However, since the Industrial Revolution over 200 years ago, the actions of people and their use of machines has had a greater and greater effect on the world's climate. Perhaps their greatest influence has been the greenhouse effect.

The amount of greenhouse gases released into the atmosphere since the Industrial Revolution has increased hugely. This is because of the increased use of cars, the clearing and burning of forests, the way people use the planet for food production, and the way people live, using appliances such as air-conditioners and heaters. The greenhouse gases that are the result of human activities rise into the atmosphere and act like a blanket to decrease the amount of radiated heat.

In Australia, scientists predict that there will be a rise in the sea levels with more floods and droughts, and the snowline in the snow field of NSW and Victoria will recede. Parts of inland Australia will receive more rainfall and the cyclone belt of Northern Australia will move further south. There is also the prediction that these changes will affect Australia's energy resources, agriculture and tourist industries. The transport we use, the way we communicate and even our health may be affected.

1. Which of the following statements is an opinion taken from the article?
   (A) The amount of greenhouse gases released into the atmosphere since the Industrial Revolution has increased hugely.
   (B) The Earth's climate has changed over millions of years.
   (C) The way we communicate and even our health may be affected.
   (D) The ice ages are an example of climatic change.

2. This article mainly uses (fact   opinion) to convince readers they should be more concerned about the environment. (Circle one answer.)

3. In your opinion, if this article was in a newspaper, would it be on the front page? ______________

4. Give a reason for your opinion. ____

5. According to the article, the main factor contributing to global warming is natural climatic change. ☐ True ☐ False

6. Global warming most likely began
   (A) when cave people began using fire.
   (B) with the invention of the motor car.
   (C) with the start of the Industrial Revolution.
   (D) when people started to use such appliances as air conditioners.

7. According to the article, how do people differ from other animals? ______________________

Relevant and Irrelevant Information

When we say something is **relevant** we are saying it is appropriate or of some importance. It has some significance. If it is **irrelevant** then it is the opposite. It is inappropriate, unimportant or insignificant. When writing, especially school assignments, only include material relevant to the topic.

It is also important to understand the relevance of information when involved in research at school. It is important to know what is relevant and what is irrelevant when we make plans to undertake certain tasks. When writing fiction (creative writing) it is important to recognise if the information is relevant to our story. Irrelevant information will make our story less appealing to the reader.

Read these instructions for playing Snakes and Ladders.

To start the game

- Put one counter for each player on START.
- Sometimes the counters are called 'men'.
- To begin playing, each player must first roll a six on the die.
- Once the player gets a six he/she rolls the die again and then moves his/her counter the number of places shown on the die.

To continue the game

- Players take turns in a clockwise direction.
- If a counter lands on the bottom of a ladder, the player moves the counter to the top of the ladder.
- If a counter lands on a snake's head, the player moves the counter to the bottom of snake's tail.
- The winner is the first person to reach FINISH.

1. Highlight the point which has the least to do with playing Snakes and Ladders.

Read part of the article 'Warbirds over Wanaka' by Shiri Gounder.

Wanaka is a scenic little town about 80 km north-west of Queenstown in New Zealand. It stays fairly dry and sunny, and despite the snow-capped peaks in the distance, temperatures remain mild. Wanaka is popular with tourists and seems to have a disproportionate number of hotels and motels.

Every two years, though, over the long Easter weekend, Wanaka's normal influx of visitors positively explodes; 75 000 people drawn by a three-day air show billed as 'Warbirds over Wanaka'.

Aviation buffs make up most of the crowd, but the display of ex-military vehicles, vintage motorcycles, farm machinery and antique fire engines has a certain appeal as well.

On the ground the vintage aircraft look spectacular. In the air, they're even more awesome, with aerial flying and stunt displays performed by the RNZAF Red Checkers and the Roaring Forties Harvard aerobatic teams.

2. If you wanted to see the air show, which one of the following facts would be least relevant?

(A) The airshow is on the Easter weekend, every two years.
(B) From Wanaka, snow-capped mountains can be seen.
(C) Stunt flying is part of the Wanaka airshow.
(D) Most visitors are interested in the vintage aircraft.

3. Select the most relevant information to illustrate the popularity of the airshow.
The Wanaka airshow's success can best be judged by (**the size of the crowd** **the weather in Wanaka** **the number of hotels**). (Circle one answer.)

4. The number of hotels in Wanaka is a direct result of the airshow. ☐ True ☐ False

5. When writing a review on the airshow, the size of Wanaka is vital. ☐ True ☐ False

Relevant and Irrelevant Information—iPhoneography

The phone is becoming the most often used camera. Of course, there are photography purists who will say your phone isn't the same as using a good camera, but the results speak for themselves. Here is a short list of guidelines.

Know your phone

Get used to your phone. If there's a way to add a shortcut that lets you fire up the camera straight away, it's a great way to make sure you don't miss those quick photos that often pass you by. If you own an iPhone you can set your home button to act as a shortcut to launch the camera. Some iPhones are very attractive.

Camera phones aren't renowned for their speed, so it's best to know the shutter speed and understand the exact moment the photo is taken.

Take note of your lighting

One of the most important things to consider when taking phone photos is lighting. Bad lighting will kill the best of pictures, even with a good camera, so when taking portrait photos with your phone, make sure your subject is well lit. If you're indoors, the photography rule of keeping the light to your back is just as important. Light behind your subject will only darken the image.

Have a steady hand

Hold your phone steady. The slightest shake could blur your image and ruin what would have been the perfect picture. Some camera apps help counteract the effect of shaking.

Avoid using digital zoom

Digital zoom is deceiving, and some phones don't even come with the feature. In essence, all digital zoom does is enlarge the image rather than zoom in, and so it immediately becomes pixelated. If you can, it's best to avoid using it and instead simply move closer to your subject.

Consider composition

Think about your photo before you take it. Take the rule-of-thirds into consideration. Many camera apps will place visible grid lines on your screen, making it easy to keep the rule-of-thirds in mind. Placing the main subjects directly along the grid lines can often lead to a stronger composition.

1. In the section *Know your phone*, highlight or underline any information that is irrelevant to the information.

2. According to the text, a portrait will be more successful if
   - ☐ it is taken with an iPhone.
   - ☐ a zoom feature is used.
   - ☐ the light is behind the photographer.
   - ☐ the subject is indoors.

3. Which of these conditions is relevant to taking 'balanced' photos?
   (A) a steady hand
   (B) using visible grid lines
   (C) using the flash facility
   (D) controlling the zoom facility

4. According to the text, phone cameras are faster than digital cameras. ☐ True ☐ False

5. Light behind the subject will ______________________________.

6. A phone photo may become more pixelated when ______________________________.

7. What do some cameras have to offset the effect of shaking? ______________________________

Relevant and Irrelevant Information—Advertisements: Iga Warta Ad

Advertisers of products are more conscious of what is relevant than many other creators of text. They must catch the reader's, viewer's or listener's attention as quickly as possible. They have limited space or time, and limited funds to promote their product and services. Every word or graphic must have some impact.

1. Referring to the ad, what is an important feature of Iga Warta? (Tick one box.)

   ☐ the food ☐ the kiosk ☐ the Aboriginal experience ☐ the hospitality

2. The location of Iga Warta is quite spectacular. ☐ True ☐ False

3. What technique does the advertiser use to make a visitor to Iga Warta feel welcome? ______________

   ____

4. Which **very relevant** piece of information is NOT included in the ad?

   ☐ how to find Copley (SA) ☐ the cost

   ☐ guides' names ☐ suitable clothing

5. What slogan is used by the advertisers? ______________

6. Facilities at Iga Warta are equal to resort standards. ☐ True ☐ False

7. What is meant by the Aboriginal word *yarta*? ______________

Understanding and Using Tables of Contents —Touch and Feeling

Most factual books have a table of contents. This is found in the front of the book, usually within the first few pages. Tables of contents are a quick reference which help readers find the main sections of the book. Some books are broken up into major chapters or topics and within each chapter, section or subject area there are subsections.

Books of fiction may also have a table of contents. These give the chapter pages or, if it is a book of many works (an anthology), the page on which individual stories, plays or poems are located.

Here is a contents table from *Touch and Feeling* by Robert Royston.

Contents

Page numbers are often in columns. In some books they are at the end of the text.

Main headings/chapters (in capitals)
Sub-headings (in lower case)

Suggested reading (Books to Read) includes other books on the same topic.

The **glossary** is an explanation of unusual words or phrases used in the book. It is in alphabetical order.

The **index** is an alphabetical list of the many topics covered in the book with their page numbers (see p. 53).

Note: some contents tables include a bibliography.

A **bibliography** is a list of books referred to in the text.

1. On what page would you find information about controlling pain? page __________
2. The bibliography is on page 30. ☐ True ☐ False
3. There are five chapters in the book. The shortest of these is ______________________.
4. The meaning of the word *angina* would most likely be found in the ______________________.
5. I want to find out about bathing a baby. What pages might give some information? ____________
6. The word *acupuncture* is used in the book. Where would I first look to find all references to *acupuncture* in the book? in the ____
7. What single word could be used to replace *Sensitive and insensitive*? ______________________

Understanding and Using Tables of Contents—The Age of Dinosaurs in Australia

by Dr Tim Flannery and Paula Kendall

CONTENTS

1. On what page will the reader find information about Lightning Ridge? page _______
2. Which section is the longest section in the book? ______________________________
3. In which section could the reader get the names of some other books on dinosaurs?

   ____
4. *Fossils* are referred to in the book. Where would I first look to find all references to *fossils*?

   in the ________________
5. To find the meaning of the word *vertebra* you would use the index. ☐ True ☐ False
6. There are two topics on page 55. ☐ True ☐ False
7. The authors referred to other books when compiling their book. ☐ True ☐ False
8. This book is mainly about dinosaurs in ______________________________.
9. Which is the better title for the book with this table of contents?

   ☐ The Age of Dinosaurs in Australia ☐ Prehistoric Terrors of Australia (Circle one answer.)

Understanding and Using Indexes— Technology for the Environment

Many factual books have indexes. They are found at the back of the book. Indexes are a quick reference which helps readers find the information in a book that is not easily found using the Table of Contents. The index items are listed **alphabetically** and give one or more pages where information may be found. References longer than one page are shown by using a hyphen (e.g. 34–37).

One of the main skills in using an index is finding the right reference word. If you wanted to find information on *rainfall* you might have to look under the entry for weather. If you don't find what you are looking for the first time try some other possibilities.

Use the index from *Technology for the Environment* by Mike Callaghan and Peter Knapp to answer the questions below.

Index

1. On what pages would you find information on animals that are *feral*? page ________
2. How many different references are there to *ozone layer* in the index? ________
3. If you wanted to find out about *recycled paper* you would look under ________.
4. How many different types of *waste* are referred to in the book? ________
5. To find out about *droughts* you will have to look under ________________________________.
6. To find information on types of *energy*, what is one entry I could try? ________________
7. The major entry for *greenhouse gases* commences on page (16 19 20 42). (Circle one.)
8. The word *salinity* means ☐ 'sliminess'. ☐ 'saltiness'. ☐ 'sample'.

Understanding and Using Indexes—Shaping the News

by John D Fitzgerald

Indexes also have their own short cuts. To save space, the main entry may not be repeated (a bit like in a dictionary). If you wanted to find out about *writing* you may have to decide what sort of writing—*writing radio news* or *writing television news*. Such sub-entries are often slightly indented.
Note: when the word *the* is part of a name or title it is usually placed last in an index entry. (See *Ashes, the* below).

Numbers in italics refer to illustrations.

Index

1. On what page would you find information about *The Age*? page ________

2. If I looked up *Yugoslavia* and went to page 14 what should I find? ____________________

3. The entry on *pictures* commences on page 24 and finishes on page ________.

4. What entry word should you look up to find information on Peter Cave? ________________

5. The entries in this index are arranged in

   ☐ order of importance. ☐ order of appearance in the book. ☐ alphabetical order.

6. An illustration for the entry *werewolf* is on page 6. ☐ True ☐ False

7. The entry *the Ashes* comes before the entry *Les Murray*. ☐ True ☐ False

8. In the book, *radio* is a more important topic than *crime* because ______________________.

9. There (is one are two) references in the index to *ABC TV*. (Circle one.)

Using Timetables—TV Guide

Timetables play an important part in our lives. Some of us use timetables for bus or train travel. We have lesson timetables at school and timetables for sports days. The program for the school concert is a type of timetable.

Timetables are a list of events according to time—when things are on. Without timetables we could be late for school! Timetables help us keep our lives in order.

A **TV guide** is a list of programmes arranged according to the time when they are screened. Use this extract from a TV guide to answer the questions below.

SATURDAY 2 December					***Western Broadsheet*** **free TV guide**		
WBN		**WTA**		**WON**		**WBS**	
Noon	Sports Clips: (includes clips from today's athletics, tennis, golf, bowls, horse racing and motor sports)	Noon	Comedy at Noon Secret Orders **G**	Noon	International Sports – discussion panel	Noon	Rage On (music)
		2.00	Regional Athletics Championships Nowra hosts the third regional championships.	1.00	Daytime Karaoke **Rpt**	1.00	Report from Brittany **Rpt**
				1.35	Far South **G** Fred follows the trails of Antarctic adventurers.	2.30	Sly Divers **G**
3.00	News Update						
3.10	Sports Scene (cont.)			3.00	Basketball Guide	3.00	Kinder Kids
		3.45	MOVIE: Amazon Ordeal (91) **Rpt G**	3.30	MOVIE: First Man Out (95) **Rpt G**	4.00	Playspace
5.00	News and Weather					5.00	Pet Vet Hotline
5.30	Good Cooking	5.30	News and Weather	5.00	Latest in Sport	5.30	Toons and Turkeys
		6.00	Armchair Sport	6.00	News at Sunset	6.30	News and Weather
6.30	Park Ranger **Rpt**	6.30	Holiday Where?	6.30	Reward: Police Files	7.00	Stop Me! **G**
7.30	Undercover Squad	7.30	Glorious Gardens **G**	7.30	MOVIE: Big Game **Rpt G**	7.30	Tourist Track **G**
8.30	Art News—Latest Exhibitions **M**	8.30	Beach Beat **PG** Sally leaves Brett.			8.30	MOVIE: Comet (Italy 06) **M S**
	Programs	**G** – General		**PG** – Parent guidance		**M** – Mature audience	
		R – Adult		**Rpt** – Repeat		**S** – Subtitles	

1. Which channel has News at 5 pm? __________
2. How long is *Far South* on WON? __________
3. Is *Art News* suitable for children? __________
4. Which channel has the most sport? __________
5. What does *PG* stand for? __________
6. When do *M* rated shows begin? __________
7. Which programme provides subtitles? ______________.
8. I need to go out at 4.30. Will I be able to watch all of *Amazon Ordeal*? __________
9. If I watched *Reward: Police Files* I would miss *Stop Me!* ☐ True ☐ False
10. The last half-hour evening news report is on at 6.00. ☐ True ☐ False
11. How long is *Sports Clips* on WBN? ______________________________
12. What programme might I watch if I were interested in motor sports? ______________________________
13. How much does this TV guide cost? ______________________________
14. Which channel appears to best cater for the interests of young children? ______________________________
15. Which movie is not suitable for children? ______________________________

Using Timetables—Bega Valley Mobile Library Service

In many country areas the library becomes mobile. The local town library uses a van to take library services to outlying areas. This three-month timetable for towns in the Bega Valley was reproduced in the local newspaper. There are no library services on public holidays (* indicates a public holiday).

Place/Town	Location	Time	Day	Sept	Oct	Nov
Merimbula	Smarties Child Care	2:30 – 3:15	Fri	11	2, 3	13
Nethercote	Near bridge	1:00 – 1:30	Mon	14	26*	16
Pambula	Preschool	10:00 – 10:45	Fri	7, 28	19	9, 30
	Beach	1:15 – 2:45	Thu	18	9, 30	20
	Toalla Rd	3:00 – 3:45	Wed	18	9, 30	20
	Pambula Public School	11:30 – 12:15	Fri	18	9, 30	20
Quaama	Near school	1:00 – 2:30	Thu	10	1, 22	12, 16
Rocky Hall	Community hall	10:15 – 12:00	Wed	16	7, 28	18
South Pambula	Near the Grange	11:45 – 12:30	Mon	7, 28	19	9, 30
Tanja	Near school	11:15 – 12:15	Tue	15	6, 27	17
Tathra	Preschool	10:00 – 10:45	Tue	15	6, 27	17
	Beach car park	1:15 – 3:15	Tue	15	6, 27	17
	Retirement village	10:00 – 11:00	Tue	8, 29	20	10
	Public School	12:45 – 2:30	Tue	8, 29	20	10
Towamba	Near school	12:30 – 2:15	Fri	4, 25	16	6, 27
Tura Beach	Near preschool	1:00 – 3:00	Tue	1, 22	13	3, 24
		11:30 – 1:30	Fri	11	2, 23	13
Wandella	Community hall	1:45 – 2:45	Wed	2, 23	14	4, 25
Wolumba	Near school	1:00 – 12:00	Tue	1, 22	13	3, 24
Womboyn	General store	2:30 – 4:30	Mon	14	26*	16
Wyndham	Public School	1:00 – 3:00	Wed	9, 16, 30	7, 21, 28	11, 18
Yowrie	Sutherland Rd	11:45 – 12:45	Wed	2, 23	14	4, 25

1. On what day does the mobile van visit Tathra Preschool? ____________________

2. This timetable is organised
- (A) in a chronological order of the times and dates various places are visited.
- (B) according to the size of community visited by the mobile van.
- (C) considering the distance the community is from Bega.
- (D) in alphabetical order of the communities.

3. Womboyn is a small community. Which fact supports this statement?
- (A) the number of visits it has each month
- (B) Womboyn's position on the list
- (C) the place where the van provides its services
- (D) the time of the day for visits by the van

4. The mobile library van goes to three public schools. They are

(A) ____________________, (B) ____________________ and (C) ____________________.

5. For how many hours is the mobile library van in Wyndham in October? ____________________

6. The Mobile van will not make any visits on October 26. Why? ____________________

7. Visits to Tathra School and Tathra Preschool are on the same weekday. ☐ True ☐ False

8. Which community has the last library visit in September? ____________________

Reading Maps—
The Oaks Town and Locality Map

We usually think of **atlases** when we think of maps. But maps can be found in many other places. Most people who live in big cities use a **street directory**. People who do a lot of travelling might use a **road map**. People interested in the universe might use a **star map**. When studying maps we are usually interested in distance and direction.

The Oaks—Town and Locality Map

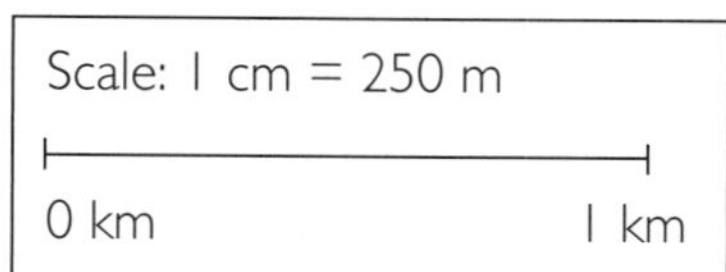

1. To go to the City from The Oaks you would have to travel to the
(A) west.
(B) north.
(C) north-east.
(D) south-west.

2. The coordinates for the Public School are
(A) E 10.
(B) F 9.
(C) G 11.
(D) F 10.

3. The Cemetery is at the corner of
(A) Mary St and Silverdale Rd.
(B) Merlin Rd and Silverdale Rd.
(C) Merlin Rd and Marle Ave.
(D) Silverdale Rd and Timothy Lacey La.

4. The coordinates for the intersection of Silverdale Rd and Browns Rd are ____________________.

5. The Reserve is between ____________________ and ____________________.

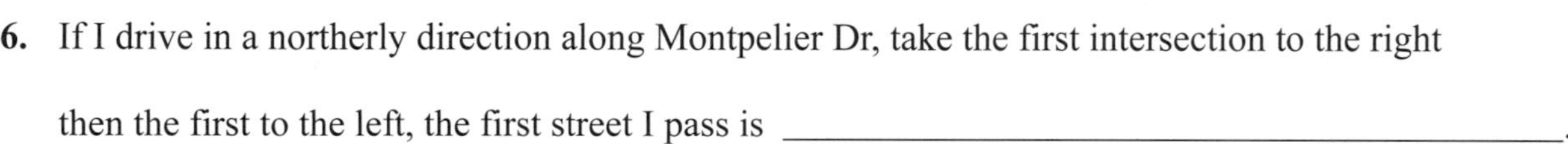

6. If I drive in a northerly direction along Montpelier Dr, take the first intersection to the right then the first to the left, the first street I pass is ____________________.

7. What are these abbreviations short for? 1. Dr. ______________ 2. Pl. ______________
3. La. ______________ 4. Rd ______________ 5. St ______________

8. About how far is it from Big Hill Rd to The Oaks Public School? ____________________

Reading Maps—Antarctica

Many countries make territorial claims to parts of Antarctica and several have permanent bases there but no-one has lived there for more than a few years. This map shows the various territorial claims to Antarctic territory and some bases.

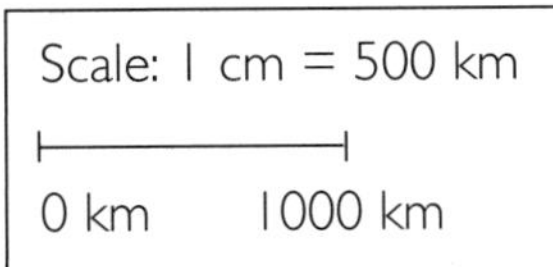

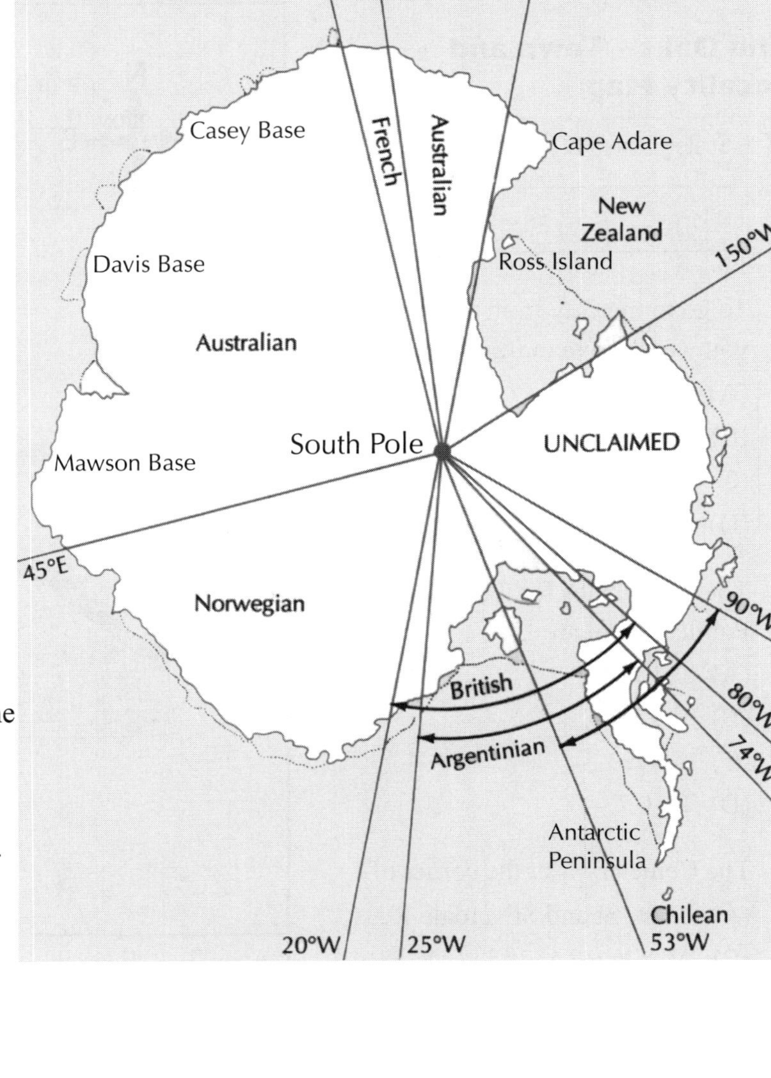

1. How many nations have claims to territory in Antarctica?

____

2. Which country has two Antarctic claims?

____

3. What is unusual about the Australian claims?

____

_______________.

4. About how far is it from the South Pole to the coast of the Australian territory following the 160° East meridian?

____

5. Approximately what fraction of Antarctica is unclaimed?
   (A) one sixth
   (B) one fifth
   (C) one third
   (D) one quarter

6. Mt Erebus is on Ross Island which is part of _______________ territory.

7. Which area has three claims on it? The area between
   (A) the meridians 25° West and 53° West
   (B) the meridians 74° West and 80° West
   (C) the meridians 20° West and 53° West
   (D) the meridians 53° West and 74° West

8. Which two countries have almost identical claims for the same territory?

_______________ and _______________

9. If I left Davis Base and went in a clockwise direction the first base I would pass would be the

_______________ Base.

Interpreting Tables, Charts and Graphs—What authors get when a book is sold

Tables, charts and graphs provide information that has to be read in a particular way. Tables, charts and graphs require you to understand how the information is presented as well as interpret the information provided.

Tables, charts and graphs are a simple way of providing information without a lot of reading.

In Mathematics you may have learned that graphs come in many forms. These include pictographs, bar or column graphs, line graphs and pie graphs. Information in books is often provided in graph form because it can save lengthy explanations. Most graphs show the relationship between two pieces of information.

These tables from the article 'What authors get when a book is sold' from *Australian Author* compare how much money an author gets from a sale in a bookshop, and how much from a sale in a book club.

Table 1—Bookshop Sales

What authors get for a book when it is sold in a bookshop RRP (Recommended Retail Price) $10.

	Approx. %	Approx. Proceeds
Bookseller	42%	$4.20
Distributor	18%	$1.80
Publisher	30%	$3.00
Author	10%	$1.00
Total	100%	$10.00

Table 2—Book Club Sales

What authors may receive when a book is sold through a book club (RRP $10—discount price $8).

	Approx. %	Approx. Proceeds
Distributor*	70%	$5.60
Publisher	26%	$2.10
Author	4%	$0.30
Total	100%	$8.00

*The book club distribution includes freight, leaflets, client servicing, packing etc in a short run turnaround.

1. According to the table, the selling of books through book clubs benefits the author more than selling through a bookshop. ☐ True ☐ False
2. In your opinion, which outlet would authors prefer for the distribution of their books? ____________. What are your reasons? ____________
3. Selling books through book clubs cuts out the need for a ____________.
4. What is the difference in return to the distributor when they sell a $10 book through a book club rather than through a bookshop? $__________
5. How much does the buyer save when buying a $10 RRP book through a book club? $__________
6. The per cent return remains much the same for the publisher whether or not the book is sold through a bookshop or a book club. ☐ True ☐ False
7. Which table shows the best return for the authors? ☐ Table 1 ☐ Table 2
8. What word in Table 2 indicates that the author's return may be less than 4%? __________
9. Who is the seller of the books under the book club sales system? __________

Interpreting Tables, Charts and Graphs—Seasons and Climate in Antarctica

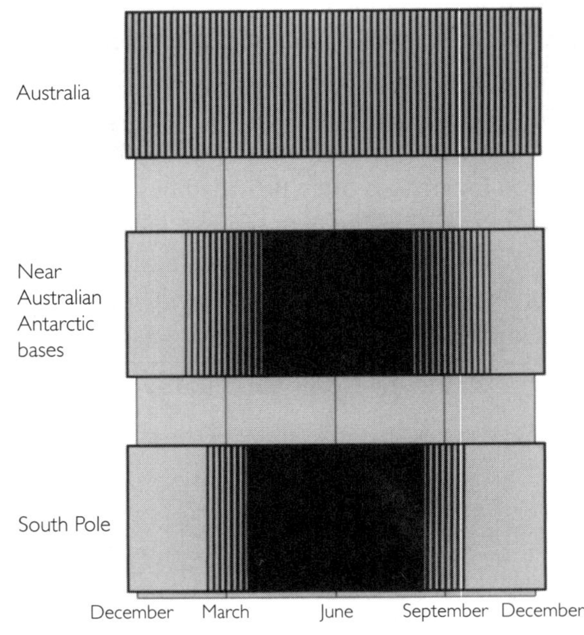

Variations between day and night in different seasons.

		Summer	Winter
Coast	highest	15	–15
	average	0	–20
	lowest (at an Australian base)	–20	–40
Inland	highest	–15	–30
	average	–30	–65
	lowest	–60	–90

Temperatures (°C) in Antarctica

Both charts from *Antarctica* by John Collerson, pp. 14–15

1. Study the two charts and choose the statement which is true.
   (A) The Australian Antarctic base has no night during spring.
   (B) The further south one travels the less daylight there is each year.
   (C) The lowest summer temperature recorded in Antarctica was – 90 °C.
   (D) The place with the coldest average temperature is inland Antarctica.

2. The ____________________ area has a temperature above freezing during ________________________.

3. It is most likely the Australian Antarctic base is situated
   ☐ at the South Pole. ☐ on the Antarctic coast. (Tick one box.)

4. What is the difference between the average temperature in winter on the coast and the average winter temperature inland? ____ °C

5. What is the difference between the highest temperature in summer on the coast and the lowest winter temperature inland? ____ °C

6. It is most likely the temperature on the coast
   (A) never rises above zero degrees.
   (B) is quite warm during summer.
   (C) is much the same in summer and winter.
   (D) can fall as low as –40 °C during summer.

7. The best season to take an Antarctic scenic flight would be ________________________________.

Interpreting Tables, Charts and Graphs—Road Casualties Graphs

Road casualties happen under a number of circumstances. The following graphs show the age distribution of people who become road casualties in a given period.

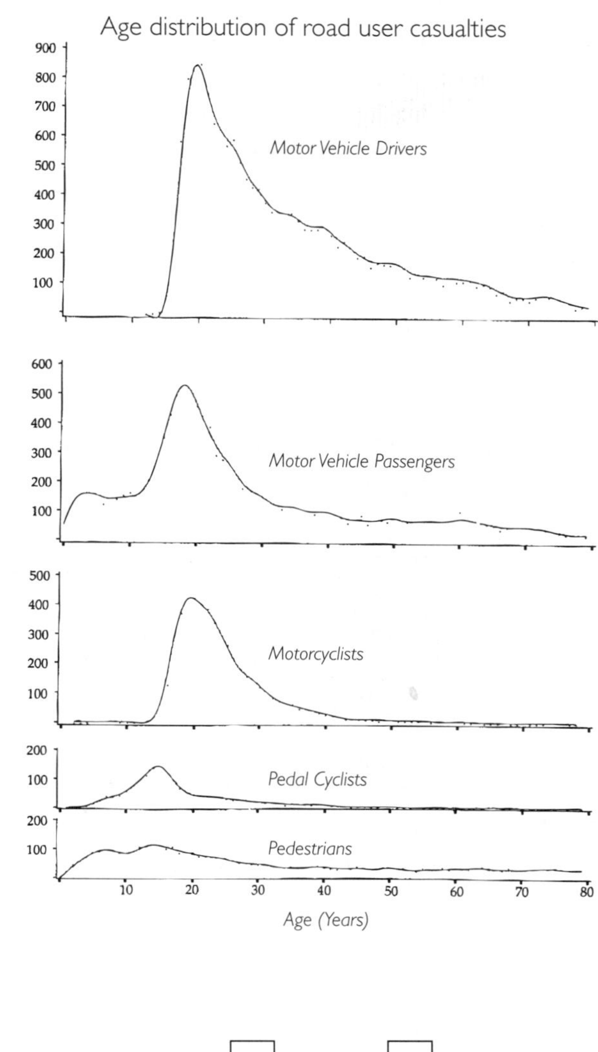

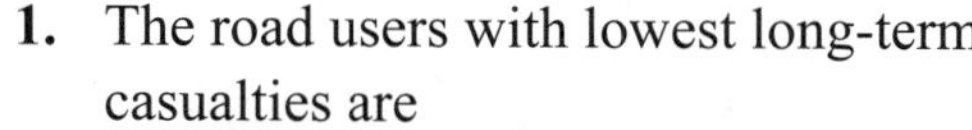

1. The road users with lowest long-term casualties are
   (A) vehicle passengers.
   (B) motorcyclists.
   (C) pedestrians.
   (D) pedal cyclists.
2. Approximately how many motorcycle casualties are 10 year olds?
   (A) five
   (B) twenty-five
   (C) fifty
   (D) one hundred
3. Overall, which age group has the most road casualties?
   (A) 5–15 year olds
   (B) 15–25 year olds
   (C) 25–35 year olds
   (D) 35–45 year olds
4. In the pedestrian group, teenagers have the highest casualty rate. ☐ True ☐ False
5. Approximately how many 20 year old drivers are involved in road casualties? ________________
6. Road casualties hardly change for pedestrians over 40. How would you explain this? ___________

   ____
7. Casualties for pedal cyclists peak with the 15 year old age group. This may be because
   (A) after 15 children get better-quality cycles.
   (B) as children get older they move to other methods of travel.
   (C) cyclists over 15 years old avoid using busy roads.
   (D) drivers become more careful when they see older children cyclists.
8. If you could make a generalisation about the information, what would you conclude? ____________

   ____

Reading Picture Narratives—For Better or For Worse

Many people enjoy comics. Comics tell stories, both short and long. They are a form of narrative. Most creators of comics use a number of techniques to tell their stories. These include:

- keeping the number of words to a minimum
- using speech bubbles for direct speech
- drawing characters with exaggerated features (which can result in some stereotyping)
- using characters to comment on social and political issues
- having a punchline (or frame).

Read the narrative in the comic strip *For Better or For Worse* and answer the following questions.

FOR BETTER OR FOR WORSE By LYNN JOHNSTON

1. The cartoonist, Lynn Johnston, has used a number of techniques to create the impression that the teenage son has spent many hours working on his computer. How is this impression created?

 ____

2. Frame 3 is an example of the character (teenage son)

 ☐ vaunting his skill. ☐ over-reacting. ☐ realising he has a problem.

3. In your opinion which character is the most obviously stereotyped? ☐ mother ☐ teenage son

 Why? ____ .

4. Comics often make use of facial features. Write down what you consider is being experienced by the mother (frame 6) and teenage son (frame 2).

 mother ____________________ teenage son ____________________

5. Comic characters often over-react or under-react. Which character, in your opinion, is the least stressed by the situation? ☐ mother ☐ teenage son

6. In the comic strip, a *virus* refers to

 (A) a stomach upset. (B) an irritating noise.
 (C) an electrical fault. (D) a computer malfunction.

7. When teenagers read this comic what conclusions might they make about parents? ____________

 ____

Reading Picture Narratives—Hagar the Horrible

1. Humour in comics often depends upon characters doing the unexpected. Which character behaves in an unexpected manner?
   (A) Hagar (the Viking warrior)
   (B) Lucky Eddy (the recruiting person)
   (C) the new applicant for a position

2. Cartoons and comics often depend upon cliché and stereotypical poses to portray their characters. Which word would best describe Hagar's interest?
   (A) involved (B) suspicious (C) unconcerned (D) disdainful

3. Comics often make use of facial features. Write down what you consider each character is mostly portraying.

   Hagar ________________ Lucky Eddy __________________ new recruit ________________

4. What impression do you get of the new recruit with his first words to Lucky Eddy?

   ____

5. The comic amuses the reader with the
   (A) strange dialogue.
   (B) Vikings' employment techniques.
   (C) repeating of a popular story.
   (D) type of clothing the characters wear.

6. Comics often comment on topical social issues. What social issue could this comic be commenting on? ____

Understanding Plot

Plot is a sequence of events in a narrative that unfolds as we read, listen or watch. Plot involves more than just sequencing events. It includes selecting the events to create an effect.

We can talk about plot in novels, short stories, verse, plays, comics and film, to mention a few. The plot of, say, many children's cartoons is pretty obvious. Something like: cat chases mouse, mouse escapes only to be chased again a little later on.

Some narratives are made more interesting with **subplots**. A subplot is a minor complication threading its way through the main story. The subplots can give depth to the main plot.

When explaining the plot of something they have read or seen, many people get 'bogged down in detail'. They haven't isolated the main events in the story.

The plot of Aesop's fable, 'The Lion and the Mouse', can be reduced to a few words.

> Mouse is caught by lion. Mouse convinces lion to let it go. Later, mouse frees lion from a trap.

The **climax** of the story is reached very quickly. The climax is the most exciting point in the story. In Aesop's fable it is when the lion seems hopelessly trapped in the hunters' net.

1. What, in your own words, is the plot of the children's story, *Goldilocks and the Three Bears*?

____

____

To make stories more interesting, there are a number of minor climaxes (**crises**) when opposing forces in the story come into conflict. (Note: crisis—singular; crises—plural)

In the story *The Three Little Pigs* these crises are easy to recognise. They happen when the wolf blows down the various houses of the three pigs until they are all trapped in the brick house of the third pig. Each crisis contributes to the impact of the climax. Things are getting worse and must be resolved by the hero! The climax comes quickly when the wolf comes down the chimney. The pigs seem trapped—until they light the fire!

2. What is the climax to the children's story, *Goldilocks and the Three Bears*? ______________

____

3. What is one of the crises in the story? ______________________________

____

Usually, it is the main character (hero/heroine) who, after a number of setbacks, triumphs or succeeds at the climax. He or she is able to resolve the problems that have been developing. This is readily observed in mystery, adventure and detective or crime stories. Often it is good triumphing over evil (**theme**).

4. Who would you consider to be the 'hero' in the fable, 'The Lion and the Mouse'? ______________

Briefly explain why. ______________________________

5. Here is the plot of a popular fable.

> Two animals decide to have a race to see who is the fastest. The faster of the two competitors gets so far ahead he decides to have a sleep. The other animal passes the sleeping competitor and wins the race.

What is the title of the story? ______________________________

6. What theme does this story have? ______________________________

Testing General Comprehension—'Indian' War Club

Here is a longer article. It brings together a number of language features included in this book. The questions following the passage will draw upon your understanding of question types you have practised and your general comprehension ability. It gives you an opportunity to test yourself.

The following story recounts the tale of three very unfortunate Lovoni (Fiji) men who were sold to the Barnum Circus in 1871. How the story came to be known is the result of investigations by Lee Parsons in 1960. At the time, Parsons was the Curator at the Milwaukee Public Museum. By researching a throwing club which turned up in the Museum, Parsons found out how it had passed through two different cultures. Parsons found the war club among Iroquois materials while dismantling a 25-year-old exhibit. Iroquois is the name given to a group of native Americans which includes the Seneca, Cayuga and Mohawk.

To Parsons' eyes the war club looked very similar to a Fijian throwing club called the ***I ula kobo***. The club was apparently made from natural roots, but this one had its root protrusions nicely rounded. Attached to the club was an eagle feather and a length of black friction tape applied to the shaft of the club.

Parsons checked the Museum's accession book and found that the club had indeed come from an Iroquois. It had been included in a large collection obtained by one of the early directors of the Museum, Dr Samuel A. Barrett.

Parsons reasoned that if the club were to lose its feather and black friction tape it would be hopelessly lost if mixed up with a group of Fijian clubs of this type. He inferred that the club itself had been picked up in Fiji, perhaps in the first half of the 19th century by a New England whaling captain or a church missionary. It was brought back to the East Coast (USA) along with other **curios** from the South Seas … the particular piece may have been traded to an Iroquois Indian along the way. The Indian would have been attracted to the object because it resembled a ball-headed war club. He enhanced the object to suit his taste by adding the eagle feather. Then, some time prior to the appearance of Dr Barrett on the scene in 1918, the shaft of the club had been repaired with American black friction tape.

Later, Parsons was given information about the history of the club from Dr Barrett, who had researched its origins.

The Iroquois Indian who had owned the club in 1918 told Dr Barrett that he had acquired the club while working in a circus. Its exact origin was unknown to him but he thought it had come from the South Seas. He had had it for a number of years and prized it because it was similar to clubs used by Iroquois in ancient times.

The investigations return to Fiji. The people of Lovoni were defeated in war by the Bau people. According to the book, 'A History of Fiji', the Lovoni people surrendered and were marched into Levuka, wasted and ___(1)___ from lack of food during a long siege. They were sold at an auction as plantation labourers to European settlers. The Lovoni land was confiscated.

It was at that auction that three unfortunate Lovoni men, including a **bete** (priest), who was a dwarf, were sold to an American circus company which featured 'Savages of the South Seas'. They were included in a side show as 'wild Fijian cannibals rescued from an enemy's pot'.

These three men probably brought the *I ula kobo* with them and gave it to the Iroquois.

1. This article could best be described as
(A) factual. (B) amusing. (C) persuasive. (D) scientific.

2. It is most likely that the three Fijian men would have found their life in a circus
(A) entertaining. (B) degrading. (C) challenging. (D) thankless.

3. Briefly retell the story of the three Fijian men. ______________________________

____

Continued over page

4. The circus treated people from primitive cultures as ______________________.

5. How do you respond to the plight of the three Fijian men from Lovoni? ______________________

6. Write 1–4 in the boxes to show the sequence in which events from the article happened.

☐ Three 'savages' are sold to the Barnum Circus.

☐ Parsons discovers a war club in an Indian exhibit.

☐ An Iroquois decorates the club with a feather and black tape.

☐ The Lovoni people are defeated by the Bau people.

7. Choose the word that would best fill the blank space (1) in the article.

(A) haggard (B) displeased (C) determined (D) troublesome

8. The word *curios*, as used in the article, has a similar meaning to

☐ souvenirs. ☐ antiques. ☐ treasures. ☐ heirlooms.

9. The war club remained undetected for many years because

(A) Lee Parsons had kept it as part of his private collection.
(B) it was part of a much larger collection of Fijian clubs.
(C) it had been adorned in a way not consistent with its place of origin.
(D) Dr Barrett had not passed on information regarding its whereabouts.

10. What conclusions do you draw about the attitudes of plantation owners to local people?

____

____

11. The writer of the article appears most fascinated by the

(A) early history of the Fijian people.
(B) efforts of Lee Parsons to solve the mystery.
(C) trading of a war club across diverse cultures.
(D) inclusion of cannibals as part of circus attractions.

12. The conflict between the Lovoni people and the Bau people took place prior to 1871.

☐ True ☐ False

13. Barnum Circus saved the Fijians from being eaten by cannibals. ☐ True ☐ False

14. What is a *bete*? ______________________

15. Where did the Fijian plantation owners come from?

16. Dr Barrett became involved in the story of the club for a second time in ______________________.

17. What is an *I ula kobo*? ______________________

18. Give one emotive (colourful) word used in the second-last paragraph. ______________________